Happiness. A Quick Immersion

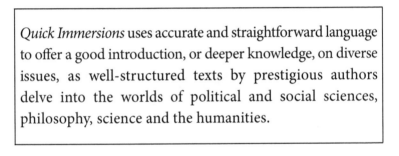

Quick Immersions uses accurate and straightforward language to offer a good introduction, or deeper knowledge, on diverse issues, as well-structured texts by prestigious authors delve into the worlds of political and social sciences, philosophy, science and the humanities.

Benjamin Radcliff and Amitava Krishna Dutt

HAPPINESS
A Quick Immersion

Tibidabo Publishing

Copyediting by Lori Gerson
Cover art by Raimon Guirado
For photograph credits, please see page 9.

First published 2019

Visit our Series on our Web:
www.quickimmersions.com

ISBN: 978-1-949845-04-4
1 2 3 4 5 6 7 8 9 10

Printed in the United States of America.

For Harolyn, Arnav and Didi

For Amy Louise, with love and gratitude

Contents

List of illustrations, tables and graphics

Introduction

It seems indisputable that happiness has always been *the* (or at least, a major) goal, or driving force, for most human beings. Much has been written in the past on the meaning of happiness and on the possibility of —and means for— achieving it. These issues have attracted the attention of religions and philosophers, given their concern with the meaning of life and on how it should be lived. Different religious and philosophical traditions from around the world have tried to understand the notion of happiness and provide guidance on how people can seek to be happy based on faith and ethics. Different disciplines, including psychology, economics and politics, have also concerned themselves with happiness, broadly defined, in connection with discussions of mental health and well-being, and what, if anything, individuals and societies as a whole can do about it. In recent years a new field of inquiry, the so-called "science of happiness," has emerged. This field tries to examine the idea of happiness using quantifiable and measurable concepts and to analyze its determinants employing the empirical and theoretical tools of the social and biological sciences. Moreover, there are numerous popular self-help books that provide advice to people on how they can become happier.

This short book on happiness seeks to provide a brief immersion into the subject of happiness by drawing on the scholarly literature on it. Among the questions it will explore are: What is the meaning of happiness? Is it something that is possible to understand in general terms, perhaps by distinguishing between different meanings of it, or is it something that is best left to people to define for themselves as they seek to be happy in their own way? Can happiness and its different meanings be measured and, if so, how? On what does happiness depend? Does a person's happiness depend on his or her disposition and individual circumstances, or does it depend in part on how society is organized and on what the government does? Does money buy happiness? What kinds of economic, social and environmental factors make people and societies happier? What can people do, either individually or collectively, to become happier?

The rest of this book proceeds as follows. Chapter 1 examines the meaning of happiness by taking a brief look at religious and philosophical traditions in history and examining what it and related ideas mean in contemporary fields of scholarship such as economics, psychology and philosophy. Chapter 2 discusses the "science" of happiness, exploring how happiness has been measured in its study and what this tells us about some of the determinants of happiness for people and societies. Chapter 3 goes into more detail on the politics of happiness, focusing on the idea of commodification. Chapter 4 examines in more detail the economics of happiness, addressing in particular the question as to whether increases in income and consumption result in increases in happiness. Chapter 5 discusses the role of social and natural environmental factors in affecting happiness. Finally, Chapter 6 examines what should be done. This is done very briefly by drawing lessons from the discussions in earlier chapters rather than as a practical guide on how to be happy. It is hoped, however, that the book will provoke people to think more about happiness and to learn more about whether, in what sense, and how people can become happier.

This book is based on the scholarly research on happiness. Constraints of space, as well as format and intended audience, make it impossible (and foolish) to attempt to provide the extensive citations that we would in a scholarly book. We have though provided essential references, which also serve as a list for further reading.

Chapter 1

What is Happiness?

Like most genuinely Great Ideas, happiness has resisted attempts to be reduced to any single meaning or definition. One useful way to understand what meanings can be attached to the word is to start with a brief discussion of how it has been used in history and by examining some contemporary scholarship on happiness and related ideas in economics, psychology and philosophy.

Philosophical and Religious Traditions

The earliest philosophers and religions in both the East and the West were concerned with the idea of happiness.

In the East (see the chapters on non-western ideas on happiness in Davis et. al., 2013), the ancient belief systems of India known as *santana dharma*, now collectively referred to as Hinduism, distinguished between different notions of happiness (with their approximate translations) including: *sukha* (happiness, ease or agreeableness), *santosha* (happiness), *harsha* (joy), *tripti* (satisfaction) and *tushti* (contentment), and *preyas* (transient happiness, instant gratification), which represent ordinary states of consciousness; and *nanda* (bliss), *stithiprajana* (abiding firmly in one's Self) and *shreyas* (well-being associated with spirituality), which represent states of happiness associated with spirituality and transcendence. However, according to *The Upanishads*, "true" happiness requires the realization of a person's oneness with *brahman*, the universal soul, and the liberation from worldly desires. As the *Katha Upanishad* states (see Easwaran, 1987):

Perennial joy or passing pleasure?
This is the choice one is to make always.
Those who are wise recognize this, but not
The ignorant. The first welcome what leads
To abiding joy, though painful at the time.
The latter run, goaded by their senses.
After what seems immediate pleasure....
Far apart are wisdom and ignorance.
The first leads one to Self-realization;
The second makes one more and more
Estranged from one's real Self.

Here perennial joy and passing pleasure are translated from the Sanskrit words mentioned earlier, *shreyas* and *preyas*. These words are spoken by Yama, or Death, and passing pleasures, obtained from wealth, material possessions and beautiful women (which Yama offers to Nachiketa, a young man), are known to be fleeting in the shadow of death. True happiness is sought through self-realization, since that self, which is the same as *brahman*, never dies. According to modern interpreters, while only a few can achieve self-realization through rigorous training in the yogas and meditation, the path to it, even in everyday life, is open to all.

Buddhism, which emerged from the teachings of Gautama Buddha between the sixth and fourth centuries BCE in India, can be interpreted as a reform movement within Hinduism. Roughly stated, one of the Buddha's insights was that ego-driven attempts to find the "true" self (self as *brahman*, the *atman*) are actually impossible, as the pursuit precludes attainment (for an accessible introduction to Buddhism and happiness, see Radcliff and Radcliff, 1993). More practically, the basic ideas of Buddhism are summarized in the so-called four noble truths: suffering exists; suffering is caused by ignorance which engenders desires, malice, pride and other mental poisons; the end to suffering is possible by removing these mental poisons; this possibility can be realized by following the path. The path, in its early formulation called the eight-fold path, involves right view, intention, speech, conduct, livelihood, effort, mindfulness and concentration, and involves training the mind to free itself of negative emotions such as desire, hatred and pride, and developing positive emotions. The latter requires recognizing that happiness depends on the happiness of others and deemphasizing oneself, and not confusing pleasure, which is fleeting and exhausted by usage and can be cruel and violent, and happiness. Some pleasures, such as enjoying nature or listening to music, need not be avoided, as long as they do not stand in the way of the search for inner freedom from suffering, of compassion, and of deep resolve to bring about a better world. How these ideas can be used today for attempting to increase happiness has been discussed by Lhamo Dondrub, the current Dalai Lama.

In China, the founders of Confucianism and Daoism, Kongzi or "Confucius" (551-479 BCE) and Zhuangzi (c.399-295 BCE), both defined happiness in terms of an objective description of the good life, but also took the view that those who attain this ideal experience a valuable sense of satisfaction, fulfillment and joy from leading such a life. However, they did not understand this as just a feeling or personal pleasures, but as an emotional state involving complex cognitions and beliefs, although not necessarily self-conscious reflection. They believed that happiness comes from following the Way, and pleasures obtained from material possessions, power and fame do not provide solid foundations of happiness.

However, they had different views of the Way, with Kongzi emphasizing family, social interactions and tradition, and Zhuangzi certain kinds of skillfulness, following the patterns and processes of Nature and aspiring only to forsake all aspirations.

The history of happiness in the Western world has been studied more systematically (see especially McMahon, 2006). In early Greek thought happiness was considered to be a matter of luck or chance. Herodotus in the fifth century BCE describes how when Croesus, the fabulously wealthy Lydian king, asked the itinerant sage and lawgiver of Athens, Solon, who is the happiest man on earth, the latter mentions the names of three men who went through many dangers when they lived but who died at their moments of glory. Croesus is surprised to learn that these dead people were happier than he was, since he considered himself happy because of his enormous wealth. But perhaps he should not have been, because tragic chance events then occur in his life soon afterwards (McMahon, 2006). Only in death is happiness assured, after which uncertainty and luck have no role. Herodotus uses several words to denote happiness, but most prominently, *eudaimonia*, which is comprised of *eu* (good) and *daimon* (god, spirit, demon), which refers to divinity and blessedness, in addition to luck. The relationship of happiness to luck and blessedness has been a theme that has continued in the West. The word happiness, in fact, is rooted in the word *happ* in Old Norse and Middle English, which means chance. The relation to blessedness continued in the Christian tradition.

In classical Greece, philosophers such as Socrates, Plato and Aristotle in the fourth and fifth centuries and the Epicureans and Stoics somewhat later took the view that *eudaimonia* or happiness is the final aim of life, which could be actively pursued by people and societies. They thus departed from the earlier Greek ideas that happiness depended only on chance, which is determined by the gods, and could be achieved, if at all, only in death. While some Greek philosophers, such as the Epicureans, did recommend increasing pleasure and reducing pain, they did not especially value everyday sensual pleasures. Thus, Plato favored the controlling of appetites rather than being enslaved by them. Aristotle valued the pursuit of the *summum bonum*, or the highest good, through virtuous living and fulfilling activities, exemplified at the highest level by intellectual contemplation, and also through friendship based on the good, rather than for utility or just pleasure, to promote human flourishing. While discussing the individual pursuit of happiness, the Greek philosophers such as Aristotle also emphasized the role of the city-state or *polis* in promoting virtuous living and human flourishing.

Christianity (as well as the other Abrahamic faiths, Judaism and Islam) regard happiness as the goal of religious life and beliefs, to be attempted through knowing and serving God. Passages in the New Testament suggest, paradoxically, that happy people are those who are hated and reviled, and those who weep, and are hungry or poor. But the concept of happiness here is not *eudaimonia*, but the Greek term *makarios*, often translated as blessed. Those who are wealthy, well-fed and full of mirth are possibly on the road to ultimate sorrow, while those who suffer unjustly in this world may rejoice. As St. Augustine expressed it, true happiness can only be achieved in afterlife, and is unattainable in a person's present life. This seems to be a return to the early Greek tradition, but the emphasis on blessedness is stronger, since true happiness in the afterlife is obtained in salvation through the union with God. Later Christian philosophers, like St. Thomas Aquinas, tried to synthesize the Aristotelian view about happiness in this world and the early Christian view that true happiness can only be achieved in afterlife by suggesting that happiness in this life, while imperfect, can approximate the true happiness of afterlife through virtuous living.

McMahon (2006) argues that the notion of happiness being our end and goal is an Enlightenment creed that has crowded out other ways of looking at the world and at human purpose in it. With the weakening of the hold of religion on everyday life and the general secularization that accompanied the Enlightenment and the Industrial Revolution, and the questioning of political absolutism and rise of egalitarian and democratic ideals, it came to be increasingly accepted that happiness is something that all people could at least aspire to in their lives on earth. It came to be accepted that suffering, injustice and inhumanity are wrong and should be reduced wherever possible, and happiness is, or should be, a basic human entitlement. Voltaire proclaimed that "Paradise is where I am," and Rousseau argued that government should try to place citizens in a position in which they can live happily, which requires a radical altering of the structure of society.

The importance of happiness is stressed in the two major political revolutions of the time, those in the United States and France. Originally drafted by Thomas Jefferson, the United States Declaration of Independence (1776) holds as a self-evident truth —in addition to the idea "that all men are created equal"— that people "are endowed by their Creator with certain unalienable rights; that among these are life, liberty and the *pursuit of happiness*" [italics added], and it is the task of the government to protect these rights. In France, the Declaration of the Rights of Man and the Citizen (1789) pledged in its preamble to "redound for happiness of all," and the Constitution (1793) proclaimed in its first article that "The goal of society is common happiness." It is ironic that the French quest for common happiness led to the Jacobin reign of terror. Less dramatically, there may also be an irony to the American pursuit of happiness. Tocqueville marveled at the ceaseless and restless effort in the United States to work hard "for fear of missing the shortest cut leading to happiness," though finally "Death steps in … it stops him before he has grown tired of this futile pursuit of that complete felicity which always escapes him" (quoted in McMahon, 2006).

Subsequent Western philosophers attached a variety of different meanings to happiness, but we can briefly discuss here just a few to illustrate. The idea of happiness as pleasure minus pain was central to ideas of the English utilitarians. For Jeremy Bentham (1748-1832) the ethical goal that government should pursue is the greatest happiness for the greatest number, although he did not see happiness as a natural right. Bentham compiled several tables of states and activities that provided pleasure and pain, and at times suggested that it is possible to calculate one's net balance of pleasure and pain, which can be called happiness. He also suggested that individual happiness can be aggregated over all people to get the society's overall level of happiness. However, at times he expressed skepticism over such precision. John Stuart Mill (1806-1873), who continued in the utilitarian tradition, distanced himself from Bentham, a friend of his father's, by explicitly arguing that some pleasures were better than others, and distinguished between contentment and happiness, where the latter referred to the pursuit of "nobler feelings," "higher" pleasures and "higher" things, which could include justice, dignity, love, self-sacrifice, beauty and liberty (McMahon, 2006). Late in life he even argued that happiness can only be attained by not making it a direct end. "Ask yourself whether you are happy, and you cease to be so. The only chance is to treat, not happiness, but some end external to it, as the purpose of life," he wrote (Mill, 1873, 117-8).

Arthur Schopenhauer (1788-1860) takes the view that optimism is not only a false, but a pernicious, doctrine because "it presents life as a desirable state and man's happiness as its aim an object." He argues that desires are illusory since they propel us to want more if we quench our desires, leading only to suffering. In these views Schopenhauer finds confirmation in, and inspiration from, the Hindu *Upanishads*, the teachings of the Buddha, and early Christian ideas. However, Schopenhauer does not argue against the possibility of happiness but, like these earlier traditions, recommends the attempt to deny the individual will and its cravings, and seek "that ocean-like calmness of the spirit, that deep tranquility, that unshakable confidence and serenity, whose mere reflection in the countenance … is a complete and certain gospel" (quoted in McMahon, 2006).

Friedrich Nietzsche (1844-1900) derides happiness, interpreted as comfort and security, as arising from the herd mentality of custom, indolence and self-preservation, taking no risks and lacking deep convictions and significant purposes. In Nietzsche's view, struggle and suffering cannot and should not be eliminated, since they generate powerful forces for overcoming obstacles and releasing creative energies that provide great joy, self-transformation and individual redemption.

It is possible to interpret these different approaches as examining happiness in terms of pleasure and pain, with utilitarians proposing the maximization of their difference, Schopenhauer (and the religious traditions) as minimizing pain, and Nietzsche as maximizing pleasure), but to do so is to miss fundamental differences in their conceptualizations of "pleasure" and "pain."

Well-being and Happiness in Economics

Economists have long tried to understand the idea of well-being and what makes people better off. Different approaches to this can be examined in terms of Sen's (1999) distinctions between the income and production, utility, and functionings and capabilities approaches to well-being.

According to the first, well-being is conceptualized in terms of income or production levels, so that increases in per capita income of a country, or the income of a person, represent increases in well-being. This approach —used by British classical economists like Adam Smith and David Ricardo and used widely to this day— is popular because of its 'objective' nature, and the fact that it can be measured in terms of money (and converted into 'real' and 'purchasing power parity' terms to take into account temporal and spatial differences in prices). However, it can be objected that it does not really represent happiness as an end, but at best provides the means to achieving it. Most mainstream economists, however, assume that individuals do the best they can according to their own reckoning (that is, maximize their utility), given their own preferences and the constraints they face, obtaining the goods and services they want and the amount of leisure time they desire. However, people may choose to do and buy things that do not end up making them as well off as they could be. This is because some things that affect them and over which they have no control change (for instance, depending on what others do and what economists call externalities), and they can make errors because of cognitive limitations, not having enough information, and because the future is uncertain —and the consequences of their actions are unknown—in the sense that there is no objective basis for calculating the probabilities of different outcomes. Moreover, other factors that depend on the environment (for instance, whether there is free healthcare) and on their own characteristics (whether they have chronic health problems) may determine how well off they can be made with a given amount of money. Finally, not everything —such as close human relationships— can be "produced" for sale by people and purchased with money.

The second approach focuses on utility, or how people feel, so that people can be taken to have greater well-being if they actually feel better off by their own reckoning, that is, their own preferences. Utility is sometimes considered to be synonymous with happiness, and is increasingly being measured in terms of surveys of subjective well-being or overall life satisfaction The advantage of this approach is that it can be affected by anything that affects a person (rather than just income) and does not rely on external standards but involves people's own (perhaps implicit) ideas on happiness. A problem with this approach, however, is that individual preferences may change over time, so that this approach uses a measuring rod the size of which may change over time. Thus, for instance, people who are poor and deprived may get used to their condition and not feel very unhappy because they adapt to their situation.

Recognizing this problem, some economists (see especially Sen, 1999) favor less subjective concepts —which is the third approach— such as functionings (whether people are able to achieve particular good results in terms of things —such as good health, adequate nutrition, and even adequate self-respect and dignity— that are considered through deliberation with others in their community and above all, with good reason, to be valuable) or capabilities (whether people have the *opportunity* to achieve these functionings, rather than whether they actually achieve them). The latter approach, which allows people to have choices, is closer in spirit to the freedom and rights-based ideas of improvements, although it adds positive rights and freedoms (such as those to obtain adequate nutrition) rather than just negative ones (those that allow people not to be restricted by the government in what they can say or do). Although these functionings and capabilities do not refer to how people feel or to their emotional state, they often are closely related to subjective feelings, and thus introduce an objective element to the notion of happiness. For instance, health promotes happiness (despite the fact that people can adapt to some health problems), and happiness can also promote good health. It is possible to view these different functionings and capabilities as components of subjective well-being (at least after careful reasoning), and they can be interpreted as reasonably objective (at least within particular communities) conceptualizations of well-being, as Sen does. Sen (1999) relate this approach to Aristotle's approach on human flourishing, that is, as providing the conditions under which individuals can flourish.

Happiness in Psychology

Psychologists have traditionally been concerned with mental disorders and illnesses such as clinical depression, bipolar disorders, anxiety disorder, and schizophrenia. More recently they have become interested in positive psychology, that is, the study of how people who do not suffer from disorders can become happier. In doing so, however, they have examined different meanings of happiness. Nettle (2005), for instance, distinguishes between different levels of happiness as examined by psychologists: a first level referring to (transient) emotions and feelings of joy and pleasure, a second referring to people's cognitive judgments and memories about their feelings over a long period of time, and a third to whether one fulfills one's true potential or whether one flourishes.

The first two levels have been referred to as scientific notions that can be measured and which do not invoke values external to the individuals who experience happiness. The first level, also called instantaneous utility, refers to how a person feels at an instant, and can be measured by having that person state, for instance, that he or she has pleasant or unpleasant feelings. If a profile of such feelings is available covering some interval of time, these instantaneous scores could be aggregated by taking a simple average for any length of time. Kahneman (1999) refers to such a concept of happiness as 'objective' happiness since, although it is based on subjective instantaneous feelings, it involves a procedure that would yield the same level of happiness for the person to any observer who has access to this happiness profile.

Since it is not practicable to obtain such profiles at infinitesimal, or even frequent, intervals, happiness measures are usually based on asking people to report on, say, a 10-point scale how happy or satisfied they are with their lives, all things considered. This approach in effect allows subjects to decide what they mean by happiness, and lets them decide how happy they are given their own definition. This approach to happiness is often referred to as subjective well-being (SWB), in an effort to apply a more precise and less emotionally laden term than happiness. While some have argued that such measures are valid and reliable, and that levels of subjective well-being and how they change over time and place can tell us about the objective conditions that make people better off, others remain skeptical because of cultural differences across people and because people are known to adapt to their environments. Thus, different cultures can interpret happiness and its desirability differently, and the poor can get used to their destitution and feel reasonably happy, as mentioned earlier in discussing the economists' notion of utility. Regardless of these possible problems, the implied notion of happiness refers to the second level of happiness. Kahneman (1999) calls it remembered utility, since it refers to what people remember about what they feel during a long period, say a year. It should be noted here that both instantaneous and remembered utility are different from decision utility, based on which – according to what is assumed by mainstream neoclassical economists – economic actors make decisions. The (decision) utility the actors expect to get after they have made their decision may not be the same as the utility they actually experience later (unless they have perfect foresight).

Kahneman (1999) argues that happiness measures based on such surveys do not measure objective happiness in his sense, because people do not remember exactly what they felt in the past, instant by instant and are, in fact, subject to many biases when they try to remember based on the heuristics they employ, such as large effects from people's current moods and conditions (because of what is called the availability heuristic). The approaches to conceptualizing and measuring happiness in other methods have been used to get closer to instantaneous happiness. One is the Experience Sampling Method (ESM), which collects information on people's reported feelings in real time as they go about leading their natural lives in real settings during selected moments of the day. Participants in studies carry handheld computers or other devices that ask them several times during a day, or several days, to answer a set of questions on the spot, including how they feel (such as happy, unhappy, depressed, angry, tired and impatient) as well as other things about where they are and what they are doing (to relate their feelings to their circumstances). This method is difficult and cumbersome to implement with large samples of people, and there is an alternative approach, called the Day Reconstruction Method (DRM), which combines elements of experience sampling and time diaries of events that occurred on the previous day and rates their feelings, possibly in terms of different adjectives (like happy, worried and angry) on a scale from, say, 0 (not at all) to 6 (very much). All this suggests that the second level is an imperfect version of something that is based on the first level, since it involves possibly faulty memories. But this is not necessarily so. As noted earlier, the second level involves more than feelings but also judgments about what a person considers to be important. A simple and trivial example of this is a soccer game in which a person is supporting a team that is ahead by a goal until close to the end of the game, when the opposing team scores two quick goals at the very end, perhaps in injury time. Objective happiness in this case may suggest that the game makes the person happy, but if he or she is mainly concerned about who wins the game, remembered happiness may be very low because of the loss. If judgments are considered to be important, level two happiness may be more appealing. But judgments can also add another problem, ast hey may depend on culture and one's environment, and on what the powerful in society "teach" them is important for happiness. Another possible difference between the two levels is the greater chance of changes in preferences or aspirations over time when examining level two happiness. This is especially the case when what is known as the Cantril scale method is used, in which a person is asked to first think about the least happy situation and give it a score of 0, and the most happy situation and give it a score of 10, and then rate his or her own happiness within that scale in the survey. It is quite possible that a person's notions of these different maximum and minimum levels, and hence the happiness score, will change over time depending on how the person's condition and happiness change over different periods.

The third level of happiness comes in different versions (see Nettle, 2005, for citations). It can refer to the Greek notion of the good life, flourishing or *eudaimonia*. It can refer to Csikszentmihalyi's idea of flow, the state one experiences when fully engrossed in an activity with a resulting loss of one's sense of place and time. It can also include Seligman's notion of authentic happiness that involves positive feelings as well as positive activities that have no feeling component (which, in any case, may be limited by a person's temperament), but make life worth living, involving wisdom, justice and authenticity, and Ryff's emphasis on personal growth, purpose in life and self-directedness, although she distinguishes it from happiness, reserving it for what can be called level two happiness. Nettle concedes that level three happiness refers to valuable things, but argues that including them in the definition of happiness makes that definition incoherent, and involves moralizing and using normative issues rather than involving people's own positive feelings or positive judgments about feelings, or what can be called "positive" psychology (no pun intended) because it involves value-free science. While this is not the place to enter into the problems with the fact-value dichotomy, it will not do to exclude a long tradition of thinking about happiness. Moreover, handing people a questionnaire or asking them to report on how they evaluate their responses to words with obscure and ambiguous meanings may be problematic, and longer-term and lasting notions of happiness as experienced by people themselves may well depend on level three happiness.

A Return to Philosophy

Given the rich discussion of happiness in philosophy, and possibly because they are not necessarily interested in concepts that allow quantification, many contemporary philosophers take a more nuanced view of happiness that distinguishes between a large range of meanings of the term happiness. A sense of these different meanings can be found from Haybron's (2008) distinctions between emotional state, hedonistic and life satisfaction approaches to happiness, as shown in Graphic 1.

The emotional state approach takes happiness to refer to a favorable emotional state. Within this approach: endorsement refers to feelings of joy and sadness, and are closely associated with gains and losses, successes and failures; engagement refers to not being bored or listless, and includes vitality — experiencing exuberance (rather being cheerful) similar to Nietzsche's notion even if not to his extreme— and flow, as discussed by Csikszentmihalyi; and attunement, which refers to inner calm and tranquility, 'somatic' confidence (feeling completely at home in one's body), and an expansiveness of mood and spirit, or simply being "uncompressed".

The hedonistic approach refers to happiness as increasing pleasure and reducing feeling unhappy, that is, cheery or 'smiley-face' feelings, but there is much more to "being happy" than "feeling" happy. This approach includes sensory pleasures and pains, while the emotional state approach refers only to what affects emotional conditions.

The emotional state and hedonistic approaches refer to feelings, but life satisfaction refers to a person's cognitive judgment about how satisfied a person is with his life as a whole but does not necessarily imply that a person has a pleasant or emotionally fulfilling life; nor does it imply that the person believes that his or her life is going well —but that it is going well enough, even if not so well or even badly.

Haybron argues that the emotional state approach is the most promising approach to, and core of, happiness. But he points out that happiness may need to go beyond it. People may often seem or feel happy, although sometimes, especially alone, they may feel and act deeply disturbed and unhappy. Beyond other kinds of emotional states, happiness can also involve virtue (otherwise, a thoughtful person may not be able to be alone with oneself and sleep at night) and a deep meaning and purpose in life (without which life can seem empty).

Whether or not one accepts these precise distinctions or prefers the emotional state approach, this discussion shows that there are many sides to happiness, and that happiness cannot be meaningfully captured by a single concept.

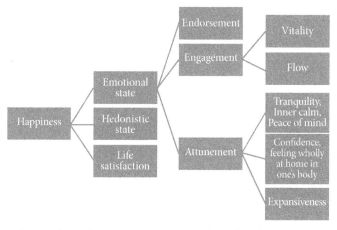

1. Approaches to happiness. Based on Haybron (2008)

Conclusion

This chapter has examined conceptions of happiness by reviewing philosophical and religious approaches, the views of economists and psychologists, and by briefly discussing recent philosophical distinctions. The main conclusion that can be reached is that happiness is a complex and many-faceted concept which defies a single, easy definition.

The next chapter will begin our exploration of the determinants of happiness. But in doing so we will focus mostly on what may be called the "scientific" approach to happiness in which "happiness" can be relatively easily conceptualized, measured and analyzed. This approach is what was referred to as the level-two approach to psychology, or what has been called remembered utility or subjective well-being. Some scholars are enamored with this approach, while others see it as being useful but also see many problems with relying on it as a single measure of happiness. Our main reason for focusing on it is that there is a vast amount of scholarly research that uses it, not least because of the increasing availability of data. However, we should remember that it is only one conceptualization and measure of happiness— albeit a useful and meaningful one— and does not capture other dimensions of happiness. To rectify this problem, we shall occasionally refer to these dimensions as well.

Chapter 2
The "Scientific" Study of Happiness

The "Scientific" Conception of Happiness

Emergence of the contemporary social scientific research program on happiness begins with the decision to leave individuals free to conceive of or define happiness however they please. The relevant question thus becomes not "what is happiness?" but rather "what makes people happy?" Thus, we do not need a definition of happiness that everyone would agree on; we must only be able to determine how happy people believe themselves to be. Once we make that transition in focus, it becomes possible to study happiness in the same ways, and using the same established canons of scientific method, that we use in the study of other human attributes.

As this approach is not concerned with what people think happiness might be, we need not ask them to define it, describe it, or tell us the path by which it can be found. We do not have to assume that the typical person even has any clear understanding of the "true" nature of happiness or has ever seriously considered its meaning. Further, in this approach we need not be able to determine if they are "really" happy using some external standard or definition imposed by the researcher. Instead, we wish to know only how people themselves feel about their lives, i.e. about how happy they believe they are in their day-to-day lives. There is now a large amount of data that tells us how happy people believe they are in response to some questions put to them by various groups of scholars and organizations, such as "All things considered, how satisfied are you with your life as a whole these days?" and "How happy are you with your life as a whole?" For now, we will not distinguish between them, but take them at face value, assuming the answers adequately reflect the respondent's level of happiness. As we are the first generation to have access to these kinds of data, we are in the enviable position of being the first to study happiness using statistical methods.

Having real data on happiness, in turn, is the open-sesame for systematic quantitative research. The process is this: once we have data on how happy people are, we can use statistical methods to find the factors that determine how happy people tend to be. Thus, we are able to deduce what issues are connected to happiness and how strong those connections are. That means we can go on to determine: What should we do to live happier lives? What life strategies, or what set of individual- and group-level strategies, are most likely to make us happy?

We can thus answer the basic question, as Albert Einstein put it, of "how should the structure of society be changed in order to make human life as satisfying as possible?" In particular, what kind of societies are most conducive to the greatest happiness for the greatest number? What would our political choices as voters be if we wished to use politics as a means to building a world in which there was more happiness for everyone? These are surely among the most compelling questions we face, both as individuals and as members of communities.

Of course, any insight we gain on these perennial questions can only be as good as the data themselves. We must realize—even stress—that reducing happiness to self-assessments is no small thing. It is not the case– as discussed in Chapter 1 - that these measures represent all there is to say about happiness: we are able to find "objective" answers about what makes people happy at the cost of using a necessarily limited definition of happiness. At the same time, we do think there is much to be learned, in that our assumptions are in fact less than might seem.

This method assumes only that there is something meaningful and interesting in knowing how happy people feel and say they are.

We do not need to assume either there is actually something called happiness or that people truly know how happy they are—instead, we only have to agree that there is something valuable and intelligible about people's subjective evaluations of their own happiness. Thus, we are not suggesting (as some do indeed maintain) that this is all there is to happiness —that is, how people say they feel when they are surveyed. Instead, we argue only what common sense suggests: that self-evaluations are not everything, but they are something, and more than that, they are something we can measure and study to good effect.

Beyond this philosophical issue, there are practical questions about the utility of subjective measures. There is, for instance, always the possibility that individuals answer questions merely because we ask them, perhaps at random or in a whimsical way. It might also be the case people do not really know how happy they are, such that their answers again do not reflect what we seek to measure. Much research has confirmed that asking questions on happiness within a research setting tends to elicit meaningful responses (e.g. Veenhoven, 1996):

- If people did not really know how to answer the questions, we would expect that the "refusal rate" on the questions would be high—that is, people would frequently refuse to answer or say that they do not know the answer. This is not the case: the refusal rate for happiness questions is not high by the standards used in survey research methodology.

- If someone does not know how to answer a question about how happy their life is, and thus answers randomly, there should be no correlation between different questions distributed throughout the survey on the same concept. For instance, if one claims to be very happy but is only answering randomly, they should also answer similar questions worded in other ways equally randomly. Thus, there should be no correlation between how happy one claims to be and, to take just two examples, how satisfying they find life to be, or how they rate their own life compared to the best possible life. In fact, we find consistent evidence that people's answers to these different questions are highly correlated, suggesting people are capturing meaningful attitudes.

- If people did not understand how happy they are, we would expect repeated measures over time to yield wildly different results, as random answering would imply. Thus, if, at time one, someone reports being very happy, but at time two claims to be extremely unhappy, without any change in life circumstances that might cause such a change, this would give us pause. Fortunately, this is not what we find: both when comparing how people answer the question early in a long interview and then again toward the end, or asking the same people over days or weeks, we find stable answers, barring obvious reasons for a change. In general, happiness measures tend to be what a statistician would call "reliable"—when asking the same question over time, we receive consistent answers.

- When we perform the same experiments, we do find, as we should, that responses do change in response to life events—life satisfaction thus declines in response to negative life events (such as becoming unemployed) and improves following positive life events (such as getting married).

- Finally, we can validate self-reported levels of happiness with external measures—for instance, that those who self-report high levels of satisfaction or happiness smile and laugh more than others, are less likely to commit suicide, are less introverted, less neurotic, less prone to worry, less pessimistic about the future, and less likely to recall negative rather than positive memories. Self-reported levels of happiness tend to match well with judgments about how happy one seems to friends and family, just as clinical evaluations of test subjects by trained psychologists are generally similar to self-reports.

- A final possibility is that people are simply dishonest in their answers, in the form of social desirability bias. Thus, respondents might feel social pressure to deny being unhappy in some countries (e.g. the United States), while in others (such as Japan) modesty might discourage claiming to be especially happy. The research again strongly suggests that this does not happen systematically. For instance, if people were dishonest in their personal reports, why would these match so closely clinical evaluations and judgments by friends and family? Similarly, attempts to find evidence of cross-cultural social desirability bias fail (e.g., those living in places where happiness is socially the most important should (but do not) show the greatest happiness, whereas those in countries where modesty is important should (but do not) systematically report the lowest amount of happiness).

Self-reported assessments of happiness—what scholars like to call "subjective well-being" (SWB)—have been subjected to a great many other tests. We need not detain ourselves with further details, as it suffices to note that these survey methods are widely agreed to provide reliable and valid data on the way people evaluate the quality of their lives. Having considered the data on happiness, we naturally come to the theories scholars have developed to explain what makes people happy.

Theories of Happiness

There are a number of possible ways to examine theories of happiness. We will discuss two such ways, one which distinguishes between mutually-exclusive overall approaches to the determinants of happiness, and the other which deals with the fulfillment of different kinds of needs.

The first starts by distinguishing between two mutually-exclusive determinants of happiness. In one, happiness is thought to be determined largely by circumstances external to the individual's inner mental processes. In this view, happiness depends on the objective, observable conditions of one's life, such as their health or income, job conditions, and whether they have a life partner and friends; by the extent to which they suffer stress, anxiety or worry caused by the possibility of unemployment or by financial insecurity; and by aspects of the society in which they live, such as crime and poverty rates. This view is sometimes associated with the idea that happiness reflects the extent to which our specific needs as human beings are met by external circumstances, with greater need-fulfillment producing greater happiness.

In the other, happiness is viewed mostly as a product of the individual's inner psychological processes, not the conditions of their lives. There is a variety of such theories. Some psychologists maintain that individuals have (perhaps) genetically determined "set points," which are like the color of your eyes: you cannot readily change them. Thus, one has a preset internal happiness level, from which people deviate only marginally, and even then, only temporarily. It is also sometimes maintained that we automatically acclimatize ourselves to whatever the objective conditions of life are through a process of adaptation, which produces much the same lack of correspondence between happiness and life conditions. In a different way, some economists also tend to focus on inner causation, believing as they so often do that happiness is determined by comparison of one's own life situation to that of others. We discuss comparison theory in more depth in a later chapter, but for the moment we need only the general idea: at least to the degree we focus on income and standard of living, people above the general level of affluence (the "consumption norm") within their society tend to be relatively happy, while those below are comparatively unhappy. If this theory is valid, attempts to raise the overall level of happiness by increasing the general material standard of living are likely to fail, in that such increases would raise the center-point around which comparisons are made.

It is important to understand the distinction between a theory that focuses on the satisfaction of human needs by changing external circumstances and other approaches. Needs-based theories correspond to our intuitive, commonsense understanding of why some people are happier than others: we are happier when more of our needs are satisfied. The happiest people are those with the greatest degree of need gratification, just as the happiest countries will be those with the institutions and structures that best allow the ordinary person to gratify their needs. We can then agree that life is better when societies are organized in those ways that best allow people to be happy. If so, to make the world a happier place, we must only identify and implement those public policies that contribute to better lives for most people (considering also that such policies do not worsen life for many others). Theories based on inner causation, alternatively, imply that since happiness is not a function of the outside world, efforts to improve living conditions will not improve levels of happiness, given that happiness is not determined by the objective conditions of life. If the degree to which we positively evaluate the quality of life depends upon internally determined set points, or if we adapt equally to whatever conditions of life we face, we cannot make people happier by changing the social or economic environment. It is not necessarily the case that people do not have needs, but these needs cannot be fulfilled by satisfying them by changing external conditions. Internal processes, however, need not imply set points, since it may be possible to alter one's inner outlook to become happier.

Equally, if we evaluate our lives through social comparison, improving living standards may not increase overall levels of happiness, in that raising the median standard of living will always leave as many people below the median as above it, and thus overall levels of happiness can never change. It should be noted that social comparison theory does not necessarily imply that social conditions cannot be changed to change the level of happiness; for instance, income inequality can be changed to do so. Moreover, if people are able to examine why they make social comparisons, they may become happier by becoming less reliant on them.

None of these approaches are intended by their more careful adherents as sole explanations of happiness, and it would be inaccurate to view them as mutually exclusive theories. The believer in genetic inheritance does not usually maintain that living conditions are utterly irrelevant, but they argue there is not much scope for improving happiness by changing them. Proponents of social comparison usually admit that only some determinants of happiness—especially incomes—operate relatively (so that many of the theory's proponents argue that the real implication is not that we should give up on greater happiness, but that we should concentrate more on matters other than income, such as economic security and stronger ties to other people), at least after some minimum needs are satisfied.

Adherents of the needs-based approach may concede that some of the variation we observe in happiness is indeed determined by set-points, genetics, or social comparison, and how 'needy' people are. We do in fact find much empirical support for each interpretation, often in ways that do not, on careful examination, entirely discredit the other approaches. It is in fact likely that our evaluation of life is determined in part by our genetic code, by social comparison, by altering how we think about happiness and what is important for us, and by the objective conditions of our lives. Individuals may have some disposition toward a certain level of happiness, as set point theory suggests, and may in some ways evaluate life relative to others, but (as we will see) this hardly negates the idea that the conditions of one's personal life situation should not affect one's happiness, any more than it discredits the view that the structure of society —the environment in which we live— is also important.

A second approach to the theory of happiness focuses on the nature of human needs and how these needs may or may not be satisfied. One of the most respected and influential attempts to enumerate human needs is that offered by the American psychologist Abraham Maslow (1943). Maslow distinguishes between five types of basic needs which motivate people to action (see Graphic 2). Physiological needs refer to those such as hunger and thirst. Safety needs refer to the need to feel secure and protected against violence, crime, extremes of temperature, illness, unemployment and financial problems. Love needs include those for affection and belonging, and are provided by family and friends. Esteem needs refer to the desire for "a stable, firmly based, (usually) high evaluation of themselves, for self-respect, or self-esteem, and for the esteem of others" and include two subsidiary sets, "first, the desire for strength, for achievement, for adequacy, for confidence in the face of the world, and for independence and freedom" and second, "desire for reputation or prestige (defining it as respect or esteem of other people, recognition, attention, importance or appreciation)."

Finally, the need for self-actualization is "the desire to become more and more what one is, to become everything that one is capable of becoming," which ranges from being based on creative urges to the desire to be an ideal parent. Based on clinical observations he also argues that these needs are hierarchically arrayed, meaning that people attend to lower-order needs first, and pursue higher-order needs only when the lower ones are fulfilled, at least to some degree. Thus, physiological needs are "the most pre-potent of all needs," which need to be satisfied, at least to some degree, before other needs, such as those for safety, and for love, are felt.

2. Maslow's Hierarchy of Needs

Maslow (1943) does not provide a rigid and mechanical theory, but notes many caveats and nuances. First, he admits that there are people whose needs may not be arranged exactly in this hierarchical order, but that it is most prevalent. Second, he does not argue that lower-order needs have to be "fully" satisfied for people to perceive higher-order ones, but may do so after they are partially met; indeed, for some people, psychological conditions may not allow their needs —such as for safety and security—ever to be met. Third, some people may be "stuck" at a lower order need and may never experience the need for, for instance, self-actualization. Fourth, he points out that the needs may be dynamic in the sense that the passage of time can affect them: people who do not achieve some needs may not feel the need strongly or at all; people who have achieved a need for a while may not be aware of the need and may even be resilient when they temporarily are prevented from achieving it. Finally, he recognizes that there are preconditions for feeling and achieving these needs, including knowledge and understanding for people, and the freedoms provided by the state and society that allow people to pursue these needs.

This need-based approach to happiness implies that people will be happy if their needs are met at least to some degree, but they may not continue being happy if new, higher needs emerge unless they, in turn, are met. It also directly suggests that people's happiness will depend positively on conditions that make people more secure, and if they have close relationships with family and friends. However, it does not tell us whether and to what extent political and economic conditions will affect happiness. For instance, having more income may satisfy biological needs, and reduce financial insecurity, and even satisfy some esteem needs by not being poor, but may not allow people to satisfy love needs, some esteem needs, and self-actualization needs.

The next logical step in the discussion is examining the main correlates of happiness as suggested by empirical studies, mostly using survey data on happiness, subjective well-being, life satisfaction and other terms which will be used synonymously for now.

Who is Happy?

The research on happiness consistently suggests that several individual-level factors influence how satisfying we find life to be. Some of these factors depend on other factors —for instance, one's race may affect one's income— and we will examine the role of these factors using studies that have focused on these factors by trying to keep other factors constant, that is, what is called "controlling" for them. Some of the most important are (for a detailed review including discussion of primary sources, see Radcliff (2013, chapter 4):

Income. Income is perhaps the most studied source of happiness. The conventional wisdom in the literature is the familiar admonition that "money does not buy happiness," in the sense that the return of income gains to life satisfaction are argued to be less than we intuitively imagine. Getting the proverbial big raise, or the big promotion, may disappoint. This point is stressed by those attempting to shift attention away from job and career and toward family and personal life, on the logic that—once we are comfortably provided for, at least—money contributes less than friends, family, hobbies, leisure, and so on. While there is indeed much to support that perspective, it is equally true that there are stark differences in happiness across income groups. In one famous study, for instance, scholars found that in the United States, "the proportion of persons rating themselves to be 'very happy' rises from 16 percent for those with incomes below $10,000 to 44 percent for those with incomes above $75,000" (Frey and Stutzer, 2002).

We see the same pattern at the other extreme: "the proportion of persons considering themselves to be 'not too happy' falls from 23 to 6 percent" when moving between these same income groups. Similar relationships apply to the UK and other developed countries. However, what is true for different people in a country is not necessarily true for the relationship between income and happiness over time and across countries, as we shall see later.

Age. Happiness is related to age in a U-shaped pattern, such that both the young and the old are happier than those in the middle. There are many reasons why this might be, the most obvious being that while youth is a source of vitality and thus happiness, it both declines over time and is diluted by the emotional costs of the frustrations and complexities of adult life, until the trend reverses in middle age as one learns how to enjoy life in a more sophisticated fashion.

Gender. On balance the collective evidence seems to suggest that, for instance, in the U.S., (a) women are marginally happier than men overall, but (b) their comparative advantage is declining. There are different interpretations as to reasons: it might be genetic or otherwise physiological, or it might only reflect the (waning?) social enforcement on traditional gender roles that equate femininity with happiness.

Race. Being non-white has the predictable effect on well-being in the United States: persons of color have lower levels of subjective well-being than whites. The magnitude of the difference between races in some studies is often much less than one might expect because some of the effects of race are absorbed by other variables, such as income, or psychological factors, such as self-esteem, both of which we might, sadly, expect to be lower among groups that have been traditionally discriminated against. It also appears that the difference between races, at least in the United States, has been declining over time, as one would hope. Cross-nationally, the data seems to suggest patterns similar in logic to the U.S. example: in South Africa, for instance, blacks report lower happiness than whites, but the difference becomes small when we control for factors (like income) which reflect their subordinate position in society.

Education. One's level of education shows less consistent effects on happiness than we might expect, but this is largely because statistical models try to isolate the independent effect of the variable in question—that is, its effect on happiness, controlling for everything else. Education is thus correlated with happiness, but the relationship is tenuous in causal terms because its affects are channeled through other variables like income. More education generally implies higher income and socio-economic status, which increase happiness; but when income and socio-economic status are controlled for, the effect of education on happiness may vanish. Some things that affect happiness, and are also affected by education, are more difficult to control for, and this can result in the finding that education reduces happiness. For instance, higher education may not provide greater happiness because it raises aspiration levels (which is not controlled for), which make it more difficult to be happy. Higher levels of education may also encourage a more obsessive and narrow interest in one's work that is detrimental to happiness—simplistically, at least, greater education is more likely to encourage individuals to think in terms of a career (rather than "just" a job) that becomes a focus of their life ambitions, lessening the energy they invest in other aspects of life, such as friends and family. Even if education has a positive influence on happiness it could be that this might not affect subjective well-being, but it may well improve the chances for increased flow, self-actualization and a meaningful and purposeful life for many.

Work. The literature confirms what common sense suggests: for those in the workforce, the quality of life as a whole is strongly affected by the quality and security of one's job. Thus, studies show that job satisfaction is a strong predictor of overall happiness. Of more interest still, students of job satisfaction have identified those aspects of work that are most important, beyond pay and benefits:

job security, physical safety at work, social status provided by the job, opportunities for personal self-direction at work, ability to actively use one's skills and abilities, non-monotony, and opportunities for friendship and other personal connections among workers. Organized workers, as will be discussed in detail in the following chapter, are happier than otherwise similar workers.

Of course, the most elemental of work related issues is employment itself, i.e. having a job. Given, as we have seen, that in market societies workers depend for their livelihoods on selling their labor power as a commodity, the inability to find a buyer for that commodity will of necessity be associated with distress. We see this clearly in the literature: being unemployed is one of the strongest correlates of unhappiness. It frequently emerges as the single most important factor in determining levels of happiness.

Social Connections. Marriage, or an equivalent form of domestic partnership, is widely agreed to be among the most important individual-level sources of happiness. The centrality of marriage requires little elaboration: at least when successful, marriage not only supplies the companionship and emotional support unique to such relationships, but also, as one scholar puts it, provides the individual an especially effective "escape from stress in other parts of one's life (in particular, one's job)."

Other kinds of personal connection also produce greater levels of well-being, with the magnitude of the effect roughly equivalent to the emotional closeness provided. Close relationships with friends or other family members would come first after marriage, followed by more casual friends, neighbors, work colleagues, and so on. All kinds of positive personal connections appear to benefit the quality of one's life, as we shall discuss further in Chapter 5.

We thus see social connections in general as being a source of happiness. Individuals who are immersed in the kinds of cooperative interpersonal networks that proponents of "social capital" are concerned with—such as social and civic clubs, neighborhood associations, and other voluntary associations— display higher levels of happiness. Social connections are also thought to promote one's abstract level of interpersonal trust—the level of trust we routinely assume of those around us—which in turn is associated with more enjoyment of life.

Social Networks. Having—or lacking—social connections of the kind noted above affect us directly and in obvious ways. But we are also affected by others in subtler and indirect ways, given happiness and unhappiness are both contagious. Much research confirms that an individual's satisfaction with life is conditioned by how happy the people one interacts with are. When your coworkers and neighbors are happy, you are more likely to be happy. In general, people are inevitably affected by the society in which they live. We are literally all in this together, insofar as happiness is concerned.

Health. As one would expect—if happiness is determined by the observable conditions of one's life—health should be closely connected to happiness. The data does indeed support the contention that health (especially self-evaluation of health) is a consistent and powerful predictor of happiness.

Religion. Attending religious services shows a positive association with happiness. The problem is that it is difficult to disentangle the social effects of attending church (which increases social connections) from a potential spiritual benefit. There are, of course, a number of ways by which religion might improve well-being, net of its effect on social connection, e.g. by providing meaning and purpose in an uncertain and dangerous world, by dampening aspirations for a better earthly life in deference to the reward of the next life, or encouraging less concern with material possessions and lessening socio-economic competition (Dutt, 2009). At the same time, though, some kinds of religious conviction can surely reduce quality of life through mechanisms too obvious and many to elaborate. In sum, the social activities of religion doubtless contribute to well-being, though we can only speculate about belief itself.

Beyond attributes of the individual person of the sort discussed above, our happiness is also affected by the conditions of the society in which we live. The most important of these include:

Economic Development and its Consequences. A nation's level of economic development is the foundation of its national level of well-being. Although —as in the case of happiness— economic development is difficult to define; life is better in many ways in rich countries than it is in poor ones, even for low income citizens. Thus, however difficult life undoubtedly is for the urban poor in the United States or the UK, there are not (yet) shanty-towns surrounding Los Angeles or London as they exist in Mexico City or Mumbai. More generally, richer countries have been argued to enjoy a background set of conditions that tend to improve life for many people: civil and political liberties; the rule of law; political stability; better levels of infrastructure; better environmental conditions; relatively accessible medical care of a relatively high quality; relatively open educational opportunities; and relatively stable economies. As one study (Frey and Stutzer, 2002: 76) observes, "It has been established that essentially all social indicators are more positive in nations of higher income: richer countries enjoy more and better-quality food, cleaner drinking water, better and more widely spread education, better health services, higher longevity, more parity between the sexes, and more respect for human rights."

Democracy. It is widely agreed that happiness is related to democracy, though there is some disagreement as to the magnitude of the relationship, its applicability beyond developing countries or those in democratic transitions, and the relative importance of democracy fostering life satisfaction vs. the reverse of satisfaction fostering democracy. Political scientists are also interested in how different kinds of democratic institutions differentially affect happiness—there is, for instance, evidence that people enjoy better lives in parliamentary (vs. presidential) democracies, and in unitary (rather than federal) systems. Evidence from the United States and Switzerland, where direct democracy is widely practiced, also suggests that the institution tends to promote well-being (perhaps especially among lower-income people whose needs are not well met through traditional party politics). In a similar vein, there is at least some reason to believe that workplace democracy, and general civic participation in the wider practice of democracy, also contribute to happier lives.

Culture. Some scholars argue that countries have "national characters," equivalent to an individual personality or set point. This view is less popular than attempts to identify specific cultural characteristics that promote or discourage happiness. Of particular interest is the idea that happiness varies between "individualistic" as opposed to "collectivist" cultures. It is argued that individualistic norms encourage citizens to pursue their own happiness as they like, whereas the collectivist orientation subordinates individual freedom to custom and conformity. This result is open to debate, primarily because the distinction between individualistic and collectivist used is problematic, failing to take into account the fact that collectivism need not imply lack of individual freedom but rather greater concern on the part of individuals for others in society. The cultural importance of tolerance has also been stressed, given that people tend to be happier in societies where "emancipative values" are most prevalent—meaning, for example, less prejudice against minorities, less rigid views toward traditional gender roles, and more acceptance of same sex relationships.

The Economy. The state of the economy obviously affects individuals, as when a recession causes incomes to fall and unemployment to grow. Less obviously, general economic conditions may indirectly affect society broadly—e.g. high unemployment will increase the level of social anxiety about potentially losing one's own job, and the secondary fears and worries that entails. These issues will be discussed further in Chapter 4. A weak economy may also encourage anti-social activities, such as crime or corruption, the generalized fear of which may again impose psychological costs on society. Finally, all these maladies are amplified by the contagion effect noted earlier: fear of unemployment or crime spread through social networks, potentially affecting a great many.

Electoral Outcomes. As discussed in subsequent chapters, there is evidence that, cross-nationally, a history of rule by labor and social democratic parties produces greater satisfaction with life than does rule by center or right parties. A similar pattern is obtained when considering rule by the Democratic Party rather than Republicans across the United States. Parties of the left contribute to human well-being because of their historical support, however tenuously and unreliably, for programs that provide vital services to everyone regardless of their incomes—such as the National Health Service in Britain or Medicare/Medicaid in the United States.

Decommodification. We discuss this issue in detail in the next chapter. For now, it is sufficient to note that the literature confirms the argument that decommodifying institutions (i.e. those that insulate individuals against the negative consequences of impersonal market forces, such as a universalistic and generous social safety net) promote well-being, net of other factors.

The natural environment. Recent research suggests that people's happiness is positively affected by the state of the natural environment in which they live, including the extent of air pollution, and the temperature. This issue will be discussed further in Chapter 5.

Conclusion

Our main purpose in the above review is expository: we want to give the reader a general sense of what we know about the determinants of happiness, and the theories scholars use (and dispute) in understanding happiness. In the two following chapters we examine political and economic factors to illustrate the mechanisms by which decommodifying public policies can affect happiness, and to see whether money really buys happiness.

Chapter 3
The Political Foundations of Happiness

No proposition in the history of political thought is less contested than the idea that the purpose of all legitimate governments is to promote the happiness of the people. Plato, for instance, argued that "our object in the construction of the state is the greatest happiness of the whole," just as Aristotle believed that we judge as "best" the government that sees to it "that every man, whoever he is, can live happily." More or less contemporaneously, the Indian political economist, Kautilya, opined that the king needs to attend to the welfare of his subjects as a matter of duty for its own sake, but also because doing so would make them happy and increase their support for him.

These echoes from antiquity, while never absent from political thought, emerged as the foundational principles of modern democracy as a result of the series of idealistic revolutions that began in the United States, France and Latin America. Today, few people would disagree with Thomas Jefferson's contention that "the care of human life and happiness…is the first and only object of good government," or John Adams's conclusion "that the happiness of society is the end of government."

We might all agree that happiness is the goal, but still lack any agreement over how the state can best foster happiness. In his characteristically incisive fashion, James Madison, the principal author of the U.S. Constitution (who was later made an honorary citizen of France for his service to universal democratic values), summarizes the fundamental dilemma of democratic politics in this way:

Good government implies two things: first, fidelity to the object of government, which is the happiness of the people; secondly, a knowledge of the means by which that object can best be attained.

It is the latter point that animates politics in the world today: we lack clear knowledge about the political means by which the object of human happiness can best be attained. What exactly should a government do—what policies should it follow—to promote happiness? What policies should we, as citizens, support if our goal was to maintain not only our own happiness, but that of our family, neighbors and society as a whole.

That project can begin by drawing on the theory which takes the view that happiness comes from fulfilling basic human needs. The lower-order needs, in Maslow's hierarchy, are primarily satisfied by economic means. We require food, clothing, shelter, healthcare and security—commodities that we can buy in a market, with money we earn by having jobs or other occupations, or which may be provided to us. We go on to strive to find and keep good jobs— those that pay well, those that are secure, those that are either inherently rewarding or tolerably enjoyable. We may well value other things more— love, friendship, and human connection above all— but economic security has the potential of making the rest of life easier: easier to love others, easier to be a good friend, easier to be a good parent, easier to find meaning and purpose in life, easier to be a kind and generous person.

As we argue below, our life chances can be seen as depending on the outcome of a political struggle consisting of two related parts. The first is between employers and employees over wages, benefits and the conditions of work. The other is the second-order conflict between classes to use the power of government—public policy—to gain advantage, including in the first arena of conflict. As we shall have occasion to see, the quality of human life across (and within) countries is in large measure determined by how these conflicts are managed and resolved. To anticipate what follows, it will become apparent that people are happiest in those societies in which ordinary working people have enjoyed the most political success. Let us thus begin by considering the nature of the forces that determine how well a given society successfully promotes the greatest happiness for the greatest number.

Commodities and Communities

At root, the conflict between Left and Right is over the appropriate strategy for addressing the social problems that emerge from what some economists and sociologists call "commodification" (see Radcliff, 2013). We will define this term presently, but must first note that our inquiry into the effects of ideological conflict on the human condition can rightly begin here not only because this is where many ideological lines are drawn, but because—to anticipate what follows—we will demonstrate empirically that a major, if not the most important determinant of the quality of life across industrialized democracies is the degree to which society has succeeded in insulating itself from the ills of commodification. Simply put, the less commodified people are, the better their lives are, other things being equal.

Commodification is a defining feature of capitalism: the vast majority of people are wage or salary workers, whose well-being depends upon selling their ability to work to those who own the productive capital of the economy. One class of people, in other words, must find jobs that are offered at the discretion of another class. On its face, that this is a fact may seem both obvious and commonplace, but its monumentality is obscured by its very ubiquity. That everyone depends for their survival on being able to sell their labor power may seem unremarkable to us, but it is a historically recent phenomenon—something fully achieved in the U.S. and Western Europe only in the last 100 years, and still an ongoing process in the developing world.

No one from before Aristotle to sometime after John Locke would have been able to understand how an entire economic system could be predicated upon the idea that our labor—the work we must all do in order to provide for ourselves and our families—could be treated like any other commodity governed by the market forces of supply and demand. They would have pointed out that there is something unique about labor that separates it from other commodities: you need to be able to sell your labor in order to feed and clothe yourself—people must work in order to survive. If their ability to work is not purchased (in the pure market society), they die. Ordinary commodities do not share this attribute: unsold cars or mobile phones, for instance, do not go off to starve to death, leaving widows or widowers and orphans in their wake.

In the world of market logic, this distinction between persons and commodities disappears.

Adam Smith is at pains to remind us of this: "The market for men is exactly the same as that for any other commodity." That people need jobs, the way they need the air they breathe, is not a relevant consideration. In the end, Smith and other apostles of the new market thinking assured us, we will be better off when we realize this. The world, they successfully argued, should be one in which someone will buy the commodity you are offering to sell (i.e. give you a job) following the same logic by which they choose to purchase any other commodity: when they themselves stand to profit by doing so. As people in this way have become just another commodity, they naturally lose the ability to make moral claims on other economic actors. While critics—sometimes including Smith himself, it must be noted—were not entirely sanguine about the implications of this transformation of the moral universe, that transformation nonetheless occurred. The Invisible Hand, the new thinking promised, would guide us all to a better world when we stopped treating other market participants as our neighbors.

What has been gained is, indeed, a more productive and vibrant economy, which over time certainly has produced a higher standard of living. But what has been lost? Thomas Jefferson summarized centuries of thought when he observed in the American Declaration of Independence that people have "natural rights," the chief of which is to life itself. If work is necessary to life, the obvious conclusion follows: one has a natural right to a job. The choice of the new market principles over this prior understanding doubtless has had many commendable consequences, but it created or exacerbated other social maladies. Two are especially worthy of note.

One is the ceaseless, inescapable insecurity that plagues a world in which nearly everyone is at the mercy of impersonal market forces. When flourishing depends on being able to sell your labor power as a commodity, and when the market for that commodity is as unstable and unpredictable as for any other commodity, perpetual anxiety is part of the bargain. Further, commodification implies that society be divided into two classes: a small group that controls access to jobs but does not need to labor themselves in order to survive, and the vast majority who depend on such people for the employment that is literally of life-saving importance. The power to decide who works and who does not is, can be referred to as, political power, although it is rooted in economic inequality. It establishes one group in a position of dominance that the other seeks to challenge. This, then, is what commodification in general produces: an economic prosperity that, while real enough, is built upon structural inequality and institutionalized insecurity, which in turn become the principal animus of political conflict.

The power differential inherent in commodification is apparent in the language invariably used to describe it, even by those who are its unequivocal advocates: workers are "reduced" to wage or salary workers, as part of the process of being "reduced" to commodities. This usage is precise and conscious, in that reduction implies a diminution of status, a loss of something once possessed. What is being lost in becoming a commodified wage laborer is independent access to a living—the ability to be able to work without being dependent on someone else to allow you to. Similarly, however well compensated, the wage laborer works for someone else, not herself. The farmer owns and works her own land and works for herself. She has a stake in and control over the whole enterprise, in the same way the partner in a law firm does. The hired farm hand, or the salaried lawyer in someone else's firm, lacks any connection to or say in the enterprise, apart from the wage she receives. Workers can, of course, save and hold wealth, from which they can earn income. However, relatively low incomes and high consumption levels (as argued in the next chapter) prevent such independence for the vast majority of workers, even in high-income countries.

This distinction between the independent owner and the dependent laborer has a long currency in political and economic thought. It takes us to the heart of the practical as well as the moral difficulty inherent in commodification: when some individuals are reduced to commodities that other people buy and sell, they cease to be persons, at least in the sense that they are no longer the political equals of the class of persons who employs them. While we must be careful not to take this too literally, the power of the metaphor can hardly be overstated. In being made dependent upon others for access to a (good) job that is necessary for a (good) life, to say nothing of when employed being treated merely as a means to other people's gain, the wage or salary worker is reduced to a lesser status, with lesser life chances.

This intellectual tradition, it must be noted, has nowhere been more revered than in the United States, however contrary to the country's anti-socialist political culture it appears. From Thomas Paine to Abraham Lincoln, we find these ideas about the dignity of labor taken as matters of faith. No one less than Thomas Jefferson, who thought the United States uniquely blessed precisely because here all could realistically achieve this dream, most famously champions this idea. Land was plentiful enough that it could be distributed (or redistributed) such that everyone who wished to could become a thriving, independent smallholder. That possibility, further, would change other economic relationships: everyone, from ordinary unskilled workers to craftsmen to accountants to clerks, would be empowered ("decommodified") by the improved bargaining position that would come from always having the option to "opt out," as it were, by seeking their fortune on the land. They would thus both be better paid and better treated by their employers. In this way, society would cease to be rigidly divided into classes, only one of which could realistically hope to be successful in their pursuit of happiness.

In the modern world, it is of course not sensible to think of providing citizens economic independence by making them all small farmers, but Jefferson's vision continues to be studied today because of its analytical power in illuminating the logic and appeal of decommodification. To further illustrate, let us consider the familiar story of the experience of British workers in the world's first Industrial Revolution. Sadly, precisely the reverse of what Jefferson envisioned occurred, but the process is the same: rather than empowering individuals by giving them the independence that comes from direct access to a livelihood, the market system stripped people of their traditional rights to the land, and with it, their independence. It reduced them to commodities.

An Illustration: Commodification in the Industrial Revolution

The Industrial Revolution evokes stark images of human suffering. Hundreds of thousands (in time, many millions) of people moved from the countryside to seek employment in the factories and mills of cities like Manchester, Liverpool and Leeds. Living conditions were notoriously dreadful—desperate people eking out a tenuous existence working for terms that no one would choose, except in the absence of any alternative. Many people lived in shantytowns with no sanitary facilities; multiple families housed themselves in equally squalid single rooms whose only furniture might be straw. Mixing poor hygiene with high population density meant that diseases such as tuberculosis and cholera were literally endemic. Malnutrition, overwork and dangerous working conditions added yet more misery.

The most vivid and memorable accounts of life at this time focus on the status of children, from which we may also deduce much about the lives of parents. As the historian Carolyn Tuttle (2001) summarizes: "children as young as five and six years old worked for twelve to sixteen hours a day, six days a week, without recess for meals in hot, stuffy, poorly lit, overcrowded factories, to earn as little as four shillings per week."

If conditions in the cities were so appalling, why did so many people leave their homes to work there? The answer, of course, is that they had to. People did not flock to the cities willingly: they were driven to do so by changes in the rural economy that made it impossible to continue living as they had. This is not the place to enter into a detailed account of this economic transformation, but it is easy enough to describe what all agree to be the single prominent cause of these migrations: the Enclosure Acts. These were parliamentary decrees designed to destroy the customary "open field system" that had historically provided a large amount of common land upon which to graze animals or raise crops. The land was common insofar as it was not fenced or "enclosed" for private use—it was the principal economic resource for much of the British population for centuries. Managed largely by the people themselves, and held as a resource for the common good, the commons were, in the words of the philosopher and sociologist Garrett Hardin, "the logical equivalent of socialism." By socialism he means that the commons were a manifestation of decommodification, providing an access to a living (farming, raising animals, crofting) without recourse to working for someone else. Removing the commons—by enclosing lands for the exclusive use of landlords—stripped an entire class of people of the basis of their economic life. While the enclosures movement was fiercely resisted, citizens were as powerless to stop it as any other aspect of capitalist development.

The destruction of the commons thus forced the movement of economically dislocated people into the only places that promised a way to earn a living: the wage-labor jobs that were abundant in the new industrial cities. Capitalism depended for its success on the development of exactly this class of people—those who, owning nothing but their ability to work, were dependent for their survival on finding a market for that labor. People went to live in the Dickensian nightmare of urban poverty because they had been dispossessed of their traditional rights to graze animals, raise crops, or otherwise work the land. They had been commodified.

The unfortunate situation of the workers perfectly illustrates what commodification means. As there was no such thing as an effective social safety net, the notion that one needed a job to survive was literally true. Nothing existed for those unable to take care of themselves—including the old, children, the sick or the injured—except the punitive, hated, near-prison of the Poor House. This was a fate so terrible, as we are reminded in the beginning of *A Christmas Carol*, the most famous of all Anglo-Saxon Christmas stories, "that many would rather die than go there." The miser villain Ebenezer Scrooge's reply that "they should do so and thus reduce the surplus population" was in fact long the official policy of the British government. The infamous 1834 New Poor Law went so far as to explicitly specify that living conditions in the Poor House be made as horrendous as possible: "Into such a house none will enter voluntarily; work, confinement, and discipline will deter the indolent and vicious; and nothing but extreme necessity will induce any to accept the comfort which must be obtained by the surrender of their free agency, and the sacrifice of their accustomed habits and gratifications."

This dismaying world, as depicted in the ordeals of *Oliver Twist*, is a model by which we can attempt to understand what life was like when there was no real recourse to finding work—any kind of work, however dangerous, degrading or low paying—if one hoped to avoid indigence or starvation. The necessity of accepting degrading, dangerous and abysmally paid work was the basis of the system, the gravity-like foundation upon which all else rested. From the point of view of cost-minimizing employers, a vast supply of desperate workers was ideal: it drove down wages and allowed one to make little provision for the safety, to say nothing of the comfort, of the employed. These shameful conditions provide great insight into the logic of the pure, raw, unfettered market—and what the human costs of the accompanying commodification can be. Without any recourse to escape the sentence of the market, life is best described by Hobbes in his account of how people lived before civilization: life was "poor, nasty, brutish, and short." We make this equation of decommodification with civilization consciously, and with deliberation. Limiting the degree to which people have become commodities does indeed further our level of civilization. As we demonstrate empirically, it is necessary for human beings to lead lives worth living.

This can be immediately seen when we consider that it is decommodification that eventually improved the life of the British working class—and by a similar political struggle, the life of working people across the entire capitalist world. A better life for the average person was achieved through more than a century of political struggle—first for the vote and then the right to organize unions, followed in time by the creation of a Labour Party to contest national elections. Those foundations established, workers concentrated on creating the first embryonic manifestations of what would later be called the welfare state. The opening years of the 20th century thus saw the first public old age pensions (1908), state funding for labor exchanges to support the unemployed (1909), and, above all, the National Insurance Act (1911), which provided free medical care and a reasonably generous system of sick pay for many millions of workers. Still, it would not be until the historic Labour Party government of 1945-1951 that a modern welfare state was finally established in the form of the National Health Service (which provided healthcare to all as a social right), a more comprehensive, universal plan of unemployment insurance, sick leave, and old age pensions (The National Insurance Act of 1946), and the establishment of a general safety net for those not otherwise in need (The National Assistance Act of 1948).

In addition—this is a point that cannot be stressed too strongly—the Labour Government formally established full employment as a central goal of economic policy. The twin goals were to effectively end unemployment as a major social problem and thus maintain upward pressure on wages. Today, conservatives frequently say that people need jobs, not government handouts. There is actually much to be said for this idea. Without digressing into a debate over whether unemployment insurance is a "handout"—given that workers make significant payroll contributions to the program with every paycheck—it is certainly true that having a job (especially a good job) can do more than any particular government program to ensure a better life. The unemployment rate is (to a significant degree) affected by governmental fiscal and monetary policy. When the government acts to maintain the lowest possible unemployment rate—it was below 3% in the UK for two decades—we not only free workers from the scourge of long-term unemployment but also create a high demand for workers that drives up wages and improves working conditions throughout the economy, as the logic of market competition implies. In this sense, full employment should be considered a path toward decommodification. The claim that government policies that aim to do this are bound to fail because there is no long-run trade-off between unemployment and inflation because of the existence of what is called the non-accelerating inflation rate of unemployment is open to serious objections (as argued in the next chapter).

These and similar policy changes precipitated a dramatic improvement in the quality of life in the United Kingdom. As no less than the Conservative opposition leader (and subsequent Prime Minister),Harold Macmillan, would tell voters when considering the Labourpolicies he vowed to maintain: "You have never had it so good." This statement serves as an excellent summary judgment of the results of the political program of the Left—as contemporary social research suggests.

It is, of course, true that the industrialization and economic growth has over long periods of time bettered the human condition. Although it has led to problems of economic instability, as experienced during financial crises and sporadic economic recessions and depressions in general, one would be foolish indeed to argue otherwise. We must be careful, though, to remember why this is. As the summary above suggests, it is emphatically not that capitalism somehow spontaneously matured into a more humane and civilized system. It is instead that citizens utilized political means—elections—to introduce a countervailing force—decommodification—into the human relations upon which capitalism is based. Having first commodified people, and thus having unleashed the productive power of capitalism, some level of decommodification was reintroduced into society in the forms appropriate to the new realities. Thus, the benefits of capitalism came eventually to be shared more equally, as decommodification improved the bargaining position of ordinary workers in their perpetual struggle for better wages, benefits, and working conditions. In the same way, and through the same mechanisms, the worst consequences of the market system have been ameliorated precisely and only by the policies of governments that were compelled by citizens to accept that at least one of their responsibilities was to see to the well-being of ordinary citizens.

The Great Transformation

The kind of economic and political changes described above are part of a more general shift in society famously described by the Hungarian-American sociologist Karl Polanyi in his hugely influential book *The Great Transformation* (1944). Polanyi argued that in the pre-capitalistic world (as is indeed now generally accepted), market forces played only a modest role in structuring either economic activity or human thought. As the market became the dominant force in economic life, it consequently also came to shape our collective understanding of the world. We thus have come to live in a dramatically transformed world— "the market society"—which must be conceived of as "a particular kind of civilization." The defining features of the market society are commodification mediated by the natural and inevitable "countermovement" for protection against the most egregious consequences of reducing people into commodities. It is this same fundamental tension between the imperatives to commodify and decommodify the individual that today animates political conflict across the world.

Most of the world lives in societies where markets have a major role. It therefore seems justifiable to think in terms of the familiar laws of supply and demand. We may even accept, for analytical purposes, the idea that individual self-interested behavior under some conditions can contribute to the common good through Adam Smith's Invisible Hand. When Smith's ideas were first articulated, Western countries still had important elements of the old (pre-market) "moral economy." The defining feature of the moral economy, according to Polanyi, was the persistence of the idea that products necessary for subsistence, at least, should be sold at fair prices, rather than at market prices. In the modern world, all things that we legally buy and sell are simply commodities. In pre-market societies, this was not always true—food in particular was thought to be decidedly different from many other commodities, given that it was, literally, of life-giving importance. Concern over its price was profoundly important, given that the vast majority of people lived on or near the knife-edge of subsistence, such that increases in the price of staples such as bread could produce great human suffering. There were accordingly strong moral proscriptions, and often legal constraints, on taking advantage of increased demand or depressed supply to raise the price of staples, on the logic that it was immoral to make greater profits that could only come from more hunger and want. In one of the famous passages from *The Wealth of Nations*, Adam Smith used the example of bread to illustrate how the new market thinking he advocated worked, as compared to the moral economy: "It is not from the benevolence of…the bakers, that we expect our dinner, but from their regard to their own interest. We [should] address ourselves not to their humanity but to their self-love, and never talk to them of our own necessities but of their advantages."

Human labor, to a degree, falls under the same umbrella. Given that one had to have a way to earn a living in order to survive, moral factors were potentially relevant in deciding when people's capacity to work could be treated just like any other commodity—to be left unbought when unneeded, and allowed to fluctuate unpredictably as demand for labor ebbed and waned. While society resisted the idea that people were mere commodities, the power of capital argued otherwise.

The expulsion of moral considerations from our assessments of economic activity was driven by the practical necessities of capitalist development—for the new system to triumph, it was necessary to reduce everything, and especially human labor, to ordinary commodities that are bought and sold in response to ordinary market forces. Still, the intellectual heavy lifting that was required to demolish the old order was, it must be remembered, driven by the sincere desire to improve life for everyone. Smith, and the similarly-minded French Physiocrats, believed that introducing market forces into those areas of human life where they were historically excluded would contribute to the common good, especially given the many government interventions resulting in monopolies recommended by the then-popular mercantilists. When food and labor are treated like other commodities, people will actually benefit, because, in the end, there would be more food and more jobs. When, in Smith's terms, we rely on the self-interest of those who wish to sell us bread or hire us to do work—when we leave the process to entrepreneurs wishing to make ever-larger profits for themselves—there will be greater abundance of both bread and work. We thus achieve better moral outcomes, it was argued, when we leave moral concerns aside. The market was to be the solution to everything: it would, as if by divine providence, lead us all to a better world. Miraculously, all that was asked of us was to follow our own selfish interests.

While Smith was certainly confident in believing, as the experience of subsequent centuries would indeed vindicate, that unleashing latent market forces would produce greater material prosperity, he was, like Polanyi, much less sanguine about the effects of the market on the human psyche. Smith was also quite aware of the fact that interests of merchants and manufacturers were opposed to those of the rest of society, since they had an inherent tendency to deceive and oppress others. For Smith, our "moral sentiments" are formed in our social relationships. When those relationships are defined through the profit-loss calculations of self-interested individuals attempting to maximize their personal gain, the effect is to coarsen and diminish the human personality. Smith argued that it was ultimately sympathy—the ability to understand and feel for others—that was the foundation of morality. He also clearly recognized that a world in which everyone would "address themselves not to their humanity but to their self-love" could only produce less empathy and thus less morality. To be sure, Smith thought that on balance the positive benefits of the market would, over time, outweigh these unfortunate effects on the human personality. Nonetheless, he believed those changes themselves to "be in the highest degree contemptible."

Such misgivings aside, the contours of the contemporary world as a market society are now apparent. Market practices and market-patterned modes of thought have established themselves as the cornerstone of modern civilization. In the new order, everyone lives under the thumb of pitiless market forces. The resulting economic system, whatever its advantages, remains one that is coldly indifferent to the lives of those who live and work within it. As Polanyi memorably put it, commodification became "the mill that ground down the lives of the people." The inevitable reaction to such a fate, he notes, is a political program of decommodification, which thus must be seen itself as a natural feature of the new market society. Commodification thus organically generates political demands for decommodification. This is the contemporary conflict between Left and Right produced by the "great transformation."

The Democratic Class Struggle

Political conflict within capitalist democracies takes place on two levels. The first is immediately familiar to us, though it is not always recognized as political: the day-to-day struggle between employees and employers over access to jobs, wages, and the conditions of work. Following Smith, we can think of economic production as the application of human labor to materials. One set of workers builds, say, the components that go into mobile phones, which another then assembles. In each instance, human labor creates something more valuable than the original materials. It is from this increase in value that both wages and profits are founded. As Smith observes "The value which the workmen add to the material…resolves itself into two parts, one of which pays their wages, the other the profit to the employer."

This process is political, in the sense that it involves power—there is a struggle between employee and employer over the value that work creates. Employees naturally wish to retain the maximum amount of value their labor has created, whereas the employer equally wishes to minimize it, to maximize his profit. Smith again provides a concise explanation of the conflict that is at the core of the market system: the wages paid workers "depends everywhere upon the contract made between the two parties, whose interests are by no means the same. The workmen desire to get as much, the masters to give as little, as possible".

Employees and employers are also in an inherently adversarial relationship in other ways. Employers decide the conditions of work, which are designed to increase productivity and profit, not to make the job comfortable or rewarding to the worker. Concessions to the preferences of workers normally will be made only when they are in the interest of (or at least not detrimental to) profitability. More generally, it is in the interests of employers to maintain control (sovereignty) in the work place, being thus at liberty to command employees to perform whatever work is desired in whatever way the employers prefer. Surrendering any portion of the power to organize work (and to discipline workers) occurs only when the bargaining position of employees is strong enough to make such demands.

We can thus conceive of work life as an arena of perpetual conflict, as worker and employer vie for position over compensation and control over the way the workplace is organized and managed. We thus assume that workers who wish to improve their position will attempt to organize, so that they can bargain collectively. Doing so improves their negotiating position, assuring that they will receive better wages and working conditions than if they had faced the employer as individuals. Employers are likely to oppose unionization for the same reasons, using whatever legal (or even illegal) powers are available to them to prevent, disrupt, or complicate organizing.

As the market society presumes a representative form of government with (in the present day at least) universal adult suffrage, both workers and employers will attempt to use the power of the state to pass laws or impose regulations that improve their position vis-à-vis the other. Workers, for instance, will press for laws that make organizing easier, while employers will seek to make organizing illegal or difficult. Workers will attempt to attack the foundation of employer power: the fact that they control access to jobs that workers desperately need in order to survive. If a country adopts a system of unemployment insurance (and otherwise funds income maintenance programs that make unemployment less intolerable) workers become less desperate. In this way, they gain both freedom and power because they do not face immediate financial ruin from unemployment, so that they are more able to take only relatively attractive jobs. Employers oppose this kind of social safety net for exactly the same reasons: workers who do not literally need jobs to survive have to be paid more and be treated better in other ways that might reduce profitability. They also oppose it since the cost of such programs are born primarily by the rich, who are more likely to receive income from profit.

Workers would also attempt to use the power of the state to provide other benefits, such as health care and pensions, in that these are things they might otherwise have to negotiate with employers to obtain. When, say, healthcare is provided to everyone as a matter of course rather than being tied to employment, workers are freed to press employers with other demands. They also fear unemployment less when they do not also face loss of access to healthcare along with their job.

In much the same way, workers seek to regulate the labor market to benefit themselves. Obvious examples are maximum working hours, mandated overtime, workplace safety rules, and so on. Employers will oppose these regulations, just as they would oppose the (high) minimum wage that workers would prefer. Employees might also press for the state to mandate paid sick and vacation days, as these might again be easier to obtain politically than through direct negotiation with employers. In this way, the group-oriented strategies of organized workers may produce benefits for everyone, as the unionized use their resources to create legal structures that benefit themselves even more by being universally available to everyone.

The battle over public policy between workers and employers forms the foundations of what has become known as the "democratic class struggle." Thus, the basic, first-order conflict of interests between employee and employer comes to find expression in a second-order conflict over control of government (so as to use the government to seek advantage, including in the first-order struggle over wages and working conditions). This, in turn, takes the form of the conventional ideological struggle between Left and Right. The initial conflict between workers and employers, an overtly class-based struggle of direct material interests, becomes subsumed in a seemingly ideational battle between abstract philosophies—and doubly so when employers are in ascendance, in that it is in their class interest as the minority party to obscure, confuse, or displace the real axis of conflict within the economy. The basic struggle between workers and employers may be further blurred when the former are too weak to organize their own political party, having to act instead as merely one interest group among many others vying for influence with the party least hostile to their interests.

To the extent party politics is organized around class interests, a main axis of conflict will be decommodification, in the three forms alluded to above: the ease by which workers can organize; the size and scope of government in general, and income maintenance programs in particular; and labor market regulations that favor workers. These are the enduring political issues in capitalist democracies. Today, the right to organize (and the ability of unionized workers to act in politics collectively) is in retreat everywhere facing conservative and neo-liberal pressures. Today, governmental austerity is the order of the day nearly everywhere, leaving the state less able to act in defense of the common interest. Today, political elites of all nominal political colors are less likely to support economic regulations designed to protect workers and consumers. What is at stake in each dispute are the class interests previously discussed, though they are disguised—however thinly—as abstract philosophical commitments that their proponents argue are best for everyone, regardless of class.

Still, both sides may be sincere in believing that their ideological program is best for society as a whole. We certainly can generalize from class interests to philosophical differences, but we must also be cognizant of the way class is a central foundation of these philosophies. Thus the Left, as the nominal agent of the working class, proposes "big government" because it thinks such policies improve the overall level of happiness in society, just as the Right, as the representative of the wealthy and business class, opposes big government, because it believes that government intervention in the economy makes life worse for everyone. But how do we actually make the intellectual leap from representing class interests to the more noble and venerated traditions of conservative and progressive thought? When moving beyond slogans and talking points, what are the abstract intellectual arguments made by the Left and the Right?

The Debate Between Left and Right

The ideological battle between Left and Right is in large part over decommodification. The Right wishes to minimize the extent to which people are freed from the necessity to labor for others in order to survive for two closely-related reasons. The less commodified people are, the less they are dependent upon the class of people who own the economy, that is, the people who have jobs to distribute. With less dependence comes more power to demand higher wages, which business will resist as inimical to profits. The Left favors decommodification through the opposite logic: the more decommodified workers are, the less they fear unemployment (or under-employment), so they can demand higher wages and better benefits.

Actual political competition, and most intellectual debate, takes place not on the desirability of decommodification itself, but on those institutions and policies that embody the principle of decommodification. Few people today are willing to object in principal to the state providing some absolute minimal level of protection from the vicissitudes of the market. Even Donald Trump argued in his campaign for the U.S. presidency that we should not "just let people die in the streets." Thus, the goal of at least some abstract minimal level of decommodification is widely accepted, with political conflict focused on the details. How and why do the Left and Right differ over these issues?

The Conservative World View

The Right believes in limiting or eliminating the safety net (and otherwise reducing the role of government); in making union organizing difficult or even (for public sector workers) illegal; and in keeping the government out of regulating the relationship between employer and employee (as in the setting of minimum wages). Putting aside the immediate question of decommodification per se, the intellectual foundation for all these positions is found in the two core ideas that animate serious conservative thought. One is the contention that the free market, left to its own devices rather than being subjected to political control, is "efficient." The other is that the same free market contributes to greater levels of human liberty, given that any effort to "tame" the market to make it more humane must ultimately depend upon coercion. While the empirical analysis that follows does not support these arguments, at least as they relate to human happiness, we by no means deny that they are worthy of attention and respect.

Efficiency is a simple enough idea. Simply stated, the market is argued to be efficient in the sense that it is Pareto optimal in the sense that it is not possible to make anyone better off by his or her own reckoning without making someone else worse off. This is sometimes stated (although not equivalently) in more simple terms as a situation which yields the greatest amount of economic output or income for given levels of human and material resources and methods of production available. This is Adam Smith's Invisible Hand once more: leave everyone to pursue in clear conscience their own individual self-interest and we conveniently arrive at the maximum level of economic output. It can be mathematically demonstrated (in what economists call "The First

Welfare Theorem") that, given certain assumptions, include individual optimizing behavior, a free market devoid of government intervention will indeed be efficient. To the extent we expect people to lead happier lives the more vibrant the economy, the efficiency standard suggests that we leave the market to itself. Attempts to change market outcomes through politics, however well-intentioned, will make society less well off, as such market interventions reduce efficiency.

Conservatives also believe that a pure market system is preferable for normative reasons. When we conceive of citizens as actors in a market (as opposed to citizens in a community), we can appeal to an elegant and normatively attractive model of the world that is predicated entirely upon free choice: there is nothing but free people making free choices in a free market. While this kind of liberty might have commendable economic consequences, we would also be wise to value it for its own sake. Liberty can be its own reward.

Few people deny that there are, at the very least, kernels of truth in both arguments. Even the most ardent critics of capitalism grant that adopting the market system contributed to a dramatic improvement in our material standard of living—and also contributed much to demolishing the archaic feudal institutions that so stifled human liberty. Marx, for instance, famously praised capitalism for freeing humanity from the "slothful indolence" of feudalism. As he notes, the result was to inaugurate an era in which capitalism would, in the span of decades, "create more massive and more colossal productive forces than have all preceding generations together." He equally celebrates capitalism's role in helping to end traditional restraints on everything from what kind of clothes people of different classes could wear to what trade they might pursue to where they might live—by, indeed, destroying all "ties that bound man to his 'natural superiors.'" The market system, whatever else one might say about it, is thus widely agreed to have achieved much of what its conservative defenders credit it with.

The conservative opposition to decommodifying practices flows naturally from this perspective. All big government programs that require substantial spending are to be avoided, in that government spending by definition is inefficient (as it is determined by political rather than market incentives). Big government, then, produces unemployment and reduces economic growth, which are both deleterious to everyone over time (as are, some would add, the deficits that democratic pressure for more government protections are likely to contribute to). Further, all such tax-and-spend policies reduce human liberty, in part because of necessity they involve redistributing wealth (i.e. confiscating the wealth of some to give it to other, and less deserving, people), and in part because of the intrusive governmental bureaucracies that result (e.g. those who are tasked, as in the British

National Health Service, with allocating medical resources through need rather than ability to pay). Thus, in sum, progressive government programs have "unintended consequences"—less economic growth, confiscatory tax policies, a bloated and uncontrollable state bureaucracy—that will overcome whatever positive contribution, if any, that such programs might make in people's lives.

Much the same is argued to be true of other political interventions in the market. Labor unions, by allowing workers to bargain collectively rather than as individuals, are argued (in Adam Smith's phrase) to be a kind of "price fixing," which is certainly contrary to the competitive spirit of the system. Unions thus distort the wage labor agreements that would have otherwise emerged, and thus again contribute to inefficiency. A minimum wage, or a prohibition on child labor, similarly interferes with the setting of wages, leading, conservatives argue, to unemployment. Similarly, setting maximum working hours, legally mandating paid sick days, or otherwise adding political criteria to employment decisions all move society away from efficiency. They may also reduce human liberty by creating (as in unions) organizations that you must join, and whose rulings you must obey, or (as in labor market regulations) by the introduction of political protocols that artificially govern issues that employers and workers would have otherwise solved "naturally" in the market.

The Progressive World View

Progressives differ from the Right above all in their rejection of efficiency as a normative standard. As they see it, maximizing the total amount of economic production is not likely to provide "the greatest happiness for the greatest number" in two respects. First, maximizing production says nothing about what is produced, and, more importantly, how it is distributed; grossly unequal distributions are likely to produce an equally unequal distribution of happiness. Second, the efficiency criteria is also silent on the nature of human relations within the market system—if (many) people feel that they are indeed treated merely as commodities, as biological machines, their well-being may suffer, however productive the economy. In sum, we as a society might well choose a less efficient system if we received in the bargain greater job satisfaction, more financial security, guaranteed access to healthcare, and a more equitable distribution of income.

Those on the Left also tend to lack faith in the even more fundamental contention that markets are in fact efficient to begin with. The most sadly vivid evidence for this is the business cycle, involving economic downturns such as the Great Depression of the 1930s and the Great Recession in the first decade of the new millennium, wherein enormous economic resources were left unused due to the lack of the demand for goods caused by business and financial investor pessimism in the presence of uncertainty about the future. Nothing could be less efficient. This is one of the insights of Keynesian economics that only a few economists now dispute. It is but a part of the Keynesian school's successful repudiation of the entire idea that the market is a self-regulating system that at any given time is making the best use of society's resources. This kind of "market failure" is accepted by many mainstream or neoclassical contemporary economists who analyze markets using optimizing individuals facing a probabilistically knowable future. To take the most conspicuous example of this intellectual trend, Joseph Stiglitz was awarded the 2001 Nobel Prize in Economics for his demonstration that "whenever information is imperfect (which is true in virtually all economies)," markets are not efficient. This contention is now widely accepted within mainstream economics, where standards of proof and verification are more widely shared than in the other social sciences. As Stiglitz (1994) observes, his work (along with that of many others) has effectively demolished whatever remained of the thin veneer of plausibility the miraculous Invisible Hand once commanded: "individuals and firms, in pursuit of their self-interest, are not necessarily, or in general, led as if by an invisible hand to economic efficiency." The phrase "market fundamentalist" has consequently emerged to describe those whose allegiance to the market is more religious-style dogma than intellectually grounded conviction.

Even the other central contention of conservatives, that free markets promote individual freedom, tells a partial story. While, free markets allow people the freedom to choose, they also allow people the freedom to lose their jobs and even their lives. Liberty does not only involve negative freedoms—to be free of constraints imposed by the government on individual actions—but also positive ones—the freedom to obtain and be things we value, such as dignity, food, and life itself, which the government may help people to achieve.

Many on the Left also worry about the effect of the market system on the human psyche. We have already alluded to the fact that the market of necessity inculcates in everyone the same self-interested, profit-loss calculus. The market encourages not only a narrow focus on one's own (and only one's own) short-term material gain, but it also provides incentives to focus on outcomes (getting what you want) rather than on the fairness or justice of the process (how you get what you want). Worse still, capitalism requires people to treat others as means to one's ends, rather than as ends themselves. Indeed, the entire basis of the economy is the ability of some people to provide needed jobs to other people only when there is a (large enough) profit to be made by doing so. In legitimating and even celebrating the successful use of other people purely as a means to one's own self-interest, the system stands in opposition to most people's ethical intuitions (whether founded in Kant or Jesus), which typically include endorsement of the maxim to "treat others as you wish to be treated."

As we have already had occasion to see, no less than Adam Smith first identified this "contemptible" effect of commodification. For Albert Einstein, this is "the worst evil of capitalism" because it stands in the way of the happiness that can only be found in fellowship with others. He argued for a reorientation of human values that he thought could be found only in what he called "socialism," meaning the European social democratic project. When our fate is at least in part affected by institutions that value people for being people, rather than being merely the product of market forces that are indifferent to us and beyond our ability to control, human life will be more satisfying. In the same way, the sociologist Max Weber concluded that the most appropriate symbol of "the spirit of capitalism" was nothing less than "an iron cage" that we must collectively escape from to find happiness. Much the same metaphor—the idea of the "market as prison"—has been employed by many thinkers, who all find the key to the door to be decommodification.

Decommodifying policies are thus at the core of progressive thought. Lacking the conservative reverence for the sanctity of the market, the Left proposes to actively use the power of the state in the way people like Thomas Jefferson advised: as an agent for furthering our collective right to the pursuit of happiness. Thus, progressives tend to favor an expansive, universalistic welfare state on the Scandinavian model—beginning with a generous system of insurance for the sick and disabled, the aged, and those otherwise incapable of finding (good) work, and continuing on to a wide range of government benefits (such as universal healthcare) and protections (high minimum wages, job security). They also recognize the importance of labor unions, both in how they protect union members per se, but also in their political contribution to public policies (discussed above) that benefit all.

Such a system, progressives believe, contributes to better lives by reducing poverty and otherwise raising living standards, by giving everyone more security (against unemployment, against illness or accident, against old age) such that people are more in control of their own lives, and by encouraging a less narrowly self-interested approach to social relationships (which is more conducive to individual happiness as well as social cohesion). It is also generally argued that these same decommodifying policies help reduce social pathologies—such as crime—that are fostered by hopelessness and desperation. Human relationships will also be nurtured, in that the less stressful, insecure and materialistic one's life is, the more one is able to devote the emotional resources necessary to sustain marriages, relationships with children and friendships.

As Joseph Stiglitz (2015) memorably notes, the fundamental goal is human solidarity:"The question is, what kind of society do we wish to live in, what kind of individuals do we wish to be? For those who support the welfare state, its central role is in creating compassionate individuals with a social conscience and with a sense of solidarity with their fellow citizens."

All of this is not to argue that state power can always be relied on to pursue these progressive objectives. The state may not always be willing or able to do so. Political leaders may try to extract as much of the economic resources as they can through corrupt and outright violent means. It can also be captured by powerful groups to serve their own class interests. For progressives, the solution to such problems does not lie in weakening the state, but strengthen it.

Happiness and Human Needs

As we have already had occasion to see, a major source of cross-national differences in happiness are differences in the objective quality of life across countries. To use the phrase popularized by the Dutch sociologist Ruut Veenhoven, we think of those societies that do a better job of offering the most people the greatest access to human needs as being more "livable." Happiness depends upon how livable one's country is (e.g. Veenohven, 2009).

We are happy to the extent we enjoy a good life, as judged by the objective conditions of what makes for a good life—such as our health or income, how much we enjoy our job, and whether we have a satisfying relationship with a life partner. The list can be elaborated to include things such as the extent to which we suffer stress, anxiety or worry (especially over finances and jobs), or various aspects of the society in which we live, such as the prevalence of injustice and poverty, and the social pathologies, such as crime, that come with injustice and poverty.

As we will see presently, the degree to which a society is livable is determined primarily by the outcome of the democratic class struggle. To see why this is true, we must begin with the specification of those needs. In Chapter 2 we discussed Maslow's approach to the hierarchy of needs. Using Maslow as a template, it is possible to draw direct connections between Left and Right public policies and the successful provision of needs. The prior discussion has in fact already given us much of the answer, which we will review here only in the briefest terms. It is obvious that policies of the Left should, from their perspective, have direct, positive connections to human needs, particularly those at the bottom of the pyramid, which are doubly important in that they have to be attained to some degree before we can reach higher-order goals. The welfare state—by which we mean, again, things like income maintenance programs, universal access to healthcare, public housing, educational opportunity and old age pensions—clearly helps to ensure that everyone has their physiological needs of food, clothing and shelter met. The welfare state also helps provide security—it reduces the enormous emotional burden the unemployed must face (the inability to provide for one's self and one's family) and even more importantly, it reduces the perpetual fear of unemployment (or underemployment) that haunts all workers, however educated or affluent.

Much the same can be said of labor unions, which should, per their proponents, contribute to greater material well-being for more people, as well as more security, in two different ways: by protecting their members per se through collective bargaining agreements, but also, and more importantly, by indirectly helping to protect all workers through their political support for decommodifying public policies that benefit everyone. Unions may also contribute to the happiness of non-members because of their political support for labor market regulations that again apply to everyone. Examples are a higher minimum wage, which raises the wage floor throughout the economy, as well as rules that promote job security and workplace safety.

Decommodifying institutions also help people to find and keep good jobs—jobs that not only pay well, but which may also be more intrinsically rewarding. It is easy to see why. The welfare state reduces the necessity of taking a job, any job, just to avoid financial ruin, as was the fate of so many during the Industrial Revolution. Employers then have to compete more for workers by offering jobs that have better pay or are more rewarding in other ways. Pro-worker labor market regulations (assuring, for instance, a safe workplace and that one will not be forced to work excessive hours) further contribute to good working conditions for everyone.

Given the hierarchical structure of needs fulfillment, these decommodifying policies arguably make it easier to obtain higher level needs. To take an obvious example, it is easier for people to maintain romantic relationships and friendships (to say nothing of connections with other family members, coworkers, etc.) when they are buffered from the stress and anxiety inherent in the fear (or reality) of poverty—or merely the day-to-day grind of an unfulfilling, poorly paid job. The role of financial stress in promoting divorce and other social problems (such as ill health, depression, alcoholism, domestic violence and suicide) is well understood. It is this simple: people who feel safe and secure in the basics of life—who have a good job, and a secure job at that—are clearly more capable of investing time and energy in these important relationships than are people who are driven (by entirely rational calculation) to focus on keeping body and soul together by clinging to a stressful, unrewarding job in the face of the even worse prospect of imminent unemployment. Individuals who have safe, secure, rewarding, well-paying jobs, in sum, will be more successful in finding (and giving) love and friendship.

Climbing another level of Maslow's hierarchy, decommodifying institutions will also contribute to higher levels of esteem. People are likely to feel respected by society when society makes some effort to treat them as valued members of a community, as reflected in income maintenance programs that combat poverty, by health policy that allows everyone access to medical care, and by rules that prevent people from being taken advantage of by employers. The fast food workers in the United States agitating for higher wages and the right to organize are a good example. What they are fighting for is recognition by society that anyone who works full-time, particularly when doing work that can hardly be thought to be anything other than drudgery, should earn a living wage. What they are asking for, ultimately, is what everyone desires: to be treated with dignity and respect. As the example illustrates, those intangibles can be found in practicalities: higher wages and the right to organize. It is also of importance to reduce the extent of income inequality since it is not just the absolute income for people, but also their relative income, which provides dignity and respect.

Self-actualization may be a nebulous idea, but it is arguable that obtaining this goal may be easier for those who have the things we have already seen decommodifying institutions provide or help to nurture: freedom from poverty and fear, a good job, strong emotional connections with others, the sense that one is a valued member of a community, and of not viewing the world in terms of monetary costs and benefits.

Arguably many on the Right also sincerely believe that their policies provide for the greatest level of need provision, but the causal mechanisms are less clear. This is because the program of the Right is predicated upon doing nothing—we are supposed to leave the market alone to let it provide the miraculous outcomes with which it is credited. To be fair, the contention is that the market is itself the causal engine by which human needs will be fulfilled, making the specification of more precise causal changes unnecessary. The liberty they believe the market fosters, presumably, will best help people provide for their own physiological needs—as will the greater economic opportunity that efficient market forces will assure without creating dependence on the state. That higher level of prosperity, coupled with the greater freedom to make one's own choices that markets imply, will do more than any governmental program to indirectly foster security, fulfilling relationships and human dignity. For the Right, the market produces a "spontaneous order" that ("as if led by an invisible hand") will create a happier world.

Empirical Evidence

Does decommodification promote or impede the pursuit of happiness? In other words, are Left or Right policies most conducive to human well-being in the sense of subjective self-reported happiness?

To approach these questions, we begin with readily interpretable understood graphical evidence, which provides simple and intuitive answers. We also review more methodologically sophisticated evidence.

Decommodification

The most obvious place to begin testing the efficacy of Left vs. Right policies is by considering how the core aspect of the welfare state—decommodification—affects satisfaction with life. Graphic 3 illustrates the basic relationship between average levels of life satisfaction over the last decade (using data from the pooled World Values Surveys) and decommodification (using the standard index of the level of social protection against unemployment from Scruggs, 2017). The WVS question asks the respondent to specify (on a 1-10 scale) "All things considered, how satisfied are you with your life as a whole these days?"

As is apparent, there is a strong, positive relationship between the variables: the line connecting them has a positive slope, such that more decommodification means more happiness. This result is statistically significant at the .001 level—meaning, the probability of finding what we do by chance is less than one in one thousand. In the graphs that follow, the reported results are also all statistically significant. As anyone can see, greater decommodification means that, on average, people find life to be a more rewarding experience.

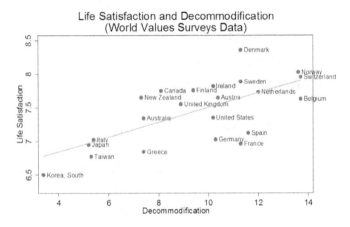

3. Life Satisfaction and Decommodification
Source: World Values Surveys Data

A skeptical reader wishing to take issue with this finding might rightly note that this kind of graphical evidence fails to consider other competing explanations for variations in happiness: i.e., how do we know it is decommodification that is causing happiness, as opposed to —for instance— some third factor driving both? As discussed in Chapter 2 and elsewhere, we know that aggregate levels of life satisfaction are affected by other things, such as the level of unemployment, the rate of economic growth, the level of per capita income, and other factors. To be confident that it is the welfare state driving happiness, we have to use statistical methods that consider these (and perhaps other) alternative explanations.

There is a great deal of scholarly research that adopts this strategy—that is, work that relies on statistical methods that allow us to separate the impact of one factor on happiness, controlling for the others, to isolate the impact of decommodification. In reviewing this research, the American political scientist Adam Okulicz-Kozaryn and his colleagues summarize by concluding that 'societies led by leftist governments (also referred to as welfare states)' have the highest levels of life satisfaction, controlling for other factors (Okulicz-Kozaryn, A. Holmes, O, Avery, 2014). This is an observation worth repeating: happiness is greatest in those countries with generous welfare states and a history of rule by "leftist" parties, net of other causes of happiness (see also O'Connor, 2017). To elaborate this conclusion, let us consider some details. The two most fundamental findings relate to decommodification per se (e.g. Radcliff, 2013):

(1) Higher levels of decommodification produce greater levels of life satisfaction, net of other factors which might also affect satisfaction. This remains true whether considering individual-level happiness or a country's average level. The welfare state contributes to greater happiness.

(2) The benefits of decommodification are the approximately the same for rich and poor. We return to this point below, but the point is worth stressing: the welfare state benefits everyone, not just the poor or the working class.

Having established that there is a well-documented statistical connection between decommodification and well-being, the next logical question is how strong is that connection? In other words, do small changes in the size and generosity of the welfare state, as we would hope, produce large changes in quality of life? The answer is an unqualified yes. The scholarly research consistently finds that the impact on the quality of one's life if moving from a country with low to high levels of decommodification (say, from Australia or the United States to the Netherlands or Scandinavia) to be substantial. The easiest way to see this is to compare this effect on satisfaction compared to the two factors universally agreed upon as being at or very near the top of the list of life events that affect happiness: marriage and unemployment. Multiple studies have shown that changing the level of decommodification as described above would produce twice as much an improvement in one's life satisfaction as getting married. The same move from a low to a high decommodification environment would provide three times the improvement in satisfaction that an unemployed person (who is normally the chief wage earner in the household) receives when finding full-time regular employment.

Radcliff, in his book *The Political Economy of Human Happiness* (2013: 129), summarizes thus:

It is worth dwelling for a moment upon how profound the effects of decommodificationare for human happiness…We need only imagine the profound psychological distress of unemployment to understand how emotionally rewardingthefindingofajobmeanstothosewho need one; we need only imagine the loneliness and isolation that comes from wishing to love and be loved—of wanting someone to share our lives with—to appreciate how fulfilling the finding of love and companionship can be. Now, consider that the effect of moving from the least to the most decommodifying welfare state would produce three times the improvement in one's quality of life than that achieved by escaping from unemployment. Or consider that this same difference in the welfare state would provide one with twice the increase in life satisfaction that finding a life-partner would. Seen in this light, it seems difficult to overstate the significance of the welfare state as an agent for human happiness.

That conclusion would be uncontestable, given that our individual level of achievements, however important, are ultimately dwarfed in their tangible impact on our happiness by structural social conditions (such as the welfare state), which are in turn determined by competitive party politics. Thus, our central conclusion: *a country's general level of happiness is determined by the choices made by voters and the governments they elect.* In particular, people demonstrably enjoy happier lives in those areas with a history of Left-party control of government, for the obvious reason that these parties are those sponsoring the decommodifying policies that help individuals lead rewarding lives (e.g. Pacek and Radcliff (2008), Álvarez-Díaz, et al. (2010), Matsubayashi and Ueda (2012)).

Other Consequences of "Big Government"

The conclusions above rely on measures of decommodification in the specific sense of protecting people from unemployment, illness or disability, or old age. We can find further evidence in favor of the basic contention of the Left or Progressive approach to politics that the more the state intervenes in the economy to help protect its citizens, the happier people tend to be. The literature suggests several, but we will consider just two.

The first is tax burden: the research confirms that a higher level of taxation (as a share of the economy) implies higher levels of life satisfaction, controlling for other factors. Clearly, no one enjoys being taxed, but higher (and especially progressive) tax burdens nonetheless do tend to promote happiness, because of what a higher tax burden provides: more and more generous government services of all kinds, including, to take just a few examples, things such as access to housing, education and healthcare; support for families and children (e.g. day care); the provision and maintenance of public infrastructure (e.g. roads, airports, mass transit, communications); and public safety—not only against ordinary crime, but also against unsafe workplaces and unsafe air, water and food. The Right may object to taxes as a matter of political taste, but it remains empirically the case that higher taxes suggest better lives for more people, in that the more resources government has, the more it can provide to the public the innumerable public goods (denoted above) that only government can provide. Note, of course, that that this is demonstrated to be true only within the context we are studying: democratically elected governments that are constrained to govern honestly by the professional and relatively corruption-free administrative apparatus presumed to exist in functional democracies. The relationship might be predictably different if these protections are lacking, such as in authoritarian or transitional countries, to say nothing of corrupt and clientalistic semi-democracies.

We come to precisely the same conclusion when considering the effect of "government consumption" on life satisfaction. Government consumption is defined as the share of the economy that the government "consumes," i.e. spends or allocates, on all activities (aside from transfers, that is, putting aside direct payments to individuals, as in pensions or unemployment benefits). Simply put, the greater the proportion of the economy that our (democratically elected) governments control, the better people find life. This evidence again suggests the superiority of Left to Right policies, in so far as we use human happiness as measured by self-reported scores as our evaluative metric. One can certainly still dislike "big government" for ideological reasons, but not for the reason that it makes life worse for the ordinary person (as it clearly does not).

Does the Welfare State Make Everyone Happier?

Suppose, as a thoughtful skeptic might suggest, that Progressive policies might raise the mean level of happiness, but only by raising the happiness floor—that is, reducing the share of the population who are the least happy, but not raising the share of people who find life to be the most gratifying. Could "big government" be guilty of subjecting our happiness to the malevolent "leveling tendencies of the masses" that preoccupied skeptics of democracy such as Alexis de Tocqueville? In this scenario, the cost of greater mean happiness would be fewer people who are the most happy, which is clearly not the optimal outcome.

This concern is addressed in Graphic 4, which shows the relationship between decommodification and the percentage of the population that has the highest possible level of life satisfaction. As is apparent, we see that the greater the size and generosity of the social safety net, the larger is the share of the population that finds life to be the most rewarding. Whatever sins one might plausibly charge to the welfare state, the data acquit it of the charge that it squeezes the pleasure out of life for some so as to give it to others. We find precisely the opposite, in fact: even if we cared only about promoting the maximum enjoyment of life by the largest share of the population (rather than the quality of the overall distribution as reflected by the mean), we would still endorse the political agenda of the Left.

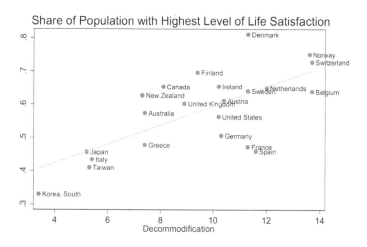

4. Share of Population with Highest Level of Life Satisfaction
Source: World Values Surveys Data

A similar fear, again close to the heart of conservatives, is this: we might be raising the mean, but only at the expense of redistributing happiness. We would thus only be redistributing happiness, not creating more of it. Thus, the welfare state might be taking happiness from the (hardworking, deserving) affluent to the (undeserving, feckless) poor. This is not the case: for both low-income (Graphic 5)) and high-income (Graphic 6) groups, we find the same strong, clear, positive, statistically significant relationships with decommodification: more decommodification means greater satisfaction. Thus, as the peer review research noted earlier also finds, we see that those with high incomes do better with greater decommodification, as do those who earn less.

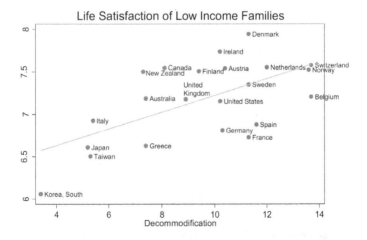

5. Life Satisfaction of Low Income Families
Source: World Values Surveys Data

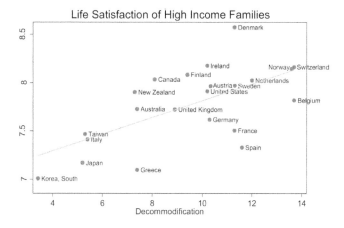

6. Life Satisfaction of High Income Families
Source: World Values Surveys Data

We have seen that the welfare state improves the lot of both the haves and the have-nots. This is no small thing, suggesting that there are not winners and losers—that we are making everyone happier, rather than taking from some to give to others. Most people find this result to their liking. The conservatives and the wealthy are comforted in knowing that however much they may disapprove of a "nanny state" playing Robin Hood with their incomes, the overall, net quality of their lives improves as the welfare state grows. Progressives and the working-class are gratified to know that the welfare programs their taxes fund really do make people's lives better—everyone, rich and poor alike. The welfare state, reasonable people might thus conclude, is like the fire department: everyone should be for it, and every responsible person should be willing to pay their fair share to fund it.

Happiness Inequality

We must briefly consider a final consequence of the welfare state: the role of the safety net in reducing inequities in the distribution of happiness. As we have had occasion to see, decommodification makes both the poor and the affluent happier, but this by no means implies that it makes happiness any more equitably shared: we could raise all boats, yet leave the absolute distance between classes untouched, or even widen it. In the contentious debate over the desirability of the welfare state, the argument that the welfare state does not (contrary to decades of inconvertible evidence) really reduce economic inequality now commands the same scientific credibility as denying climate change, but it just might be possible to argue that the welfare state fails in its goal of reducing inequality if we think in terms of happiness rather than income. Progressives, too, have a stake in believing that we should be striving not merely for a more equal distribution of income, but also an equal distribution of good lives.

It is easy to compute a measure of inequality in life satisfaction: we merely apply to the distribution of happiness the same mathematical formula that gives us the most commonly used measure of the distribution of income: the "Gini coefficient." The Gini theoretically ranges from zero to one. At zero, there is complete equality, in that everyone has the same amount of happiness; at 1.0 there is complete inequality, i.e. all happiness is (so to speak) possessed by a single person. For our purposes, we need only remember that higher values mean greater inequality. Since people evaluate happiness levels according to their own scales, the levels of happiness for different people are not, strictly speaking, comparable, so that *levels* of inequality are not meaningful by this measure. However, *variations* in the measure across countries or over time can still provide meaningful information.

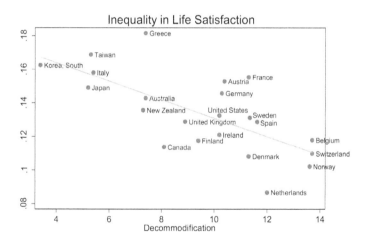

7. Inequality in Life Satisfaction
Source: World Values Surveys Data

The relationship between happiness-inequality and decommodification is illustrated in Graphic 7. As is apparent, there we have a line with a negative (downward) slope, suggesting of course that as decommodification increases, the inequality of happiness decreases.

Labor Unions and Happiness

Earlier in this chapter we introduced the argument that labor unions improve the quality of life for everyone in society—members and non-members, low incomes and high incomes. We will not repeat that discussion here, but content ourselves with demonstrating as briefly as possible its empirical veracity (e.g. Flavin, et al. (2010), Radcliff (2013)).

A good beginning is Graphic 8. Here we see that the relationship between labor union density (the share of workers who belong to unions) and the average level of life satisfaction conform to our expectations: more workers in unions suggests greater happiness.

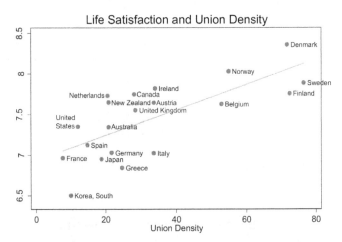

8. Life Satisfaction and Union Density
Source: World Values Surveys Data

As with prior graphical evidence, these results are only suggestive, as they fail to control for alternative factors (among other statistical details), but again the peer reviewed scholarly research comes to the same conclusion. Two lines of research are worth noting. One shows that union members are happier than otherwise similar others—people who belong to unions are thus happier than others of the same age and gender, with the same income and marital status, and so on. Belonging to a union makes people happy.

The second considers the impact of labor union density on society as a whole. Here, the argument is not about being a member of a union, but of living in a society where unions are strong. A strong labor movement tends to work to the benefit of working people in general, not just union members, in that the political power of unions (as noted earlier) helps support decommodifying policies (such as the welfare state) and labor market regulations (such as a high minimum wage) that work to the benefit of most. The literature confirms these expectations, though it suggests that of the two mechanisms by which unions improve happiness, the strongest effects are through high union density. The predicted change in happiness when moving from very-low to a very-high density country is just slightly less pronounced than those noted above when comparing low- to high-decommodification environments. Critically, the benefits of greater union density can be demonstrated, as expected, to apply to those who are not members of unions (thus, for instance, Graphic 8 looks almost identical when considering only union members vs. non-members).

In sum: the empirical evidence confirms our theoretical expectations about the beneficent effects of labor organization on the quality of human life. Unions make life better for everyone, regardless of whether or not they belong to a union.

Conclusion

The theoretical and empirical arguments advanced in this chapter do not require further review or elaboration. The data on human well-being could not speak more eloquently about what we, as citizens, should do, in so far as we care about promoting the greatest good for the greatest number. Both the average level of happiness and the share of the population that finds life to be the most satisfying are best furthered by a generous, universalistic social safety net. This chapter has demonstrated, repeatedly, in different ways, that the welfare state, and other aspects of "big government," dramatically improve quality of life for everyone, rich as well as poor. Strong labor unions play a similar role: the more workers who belong to unions, the happier people areas measured by subjective or self-reported happiness scores, whether they themselves belong to a union or not, and regardless of their income. Decommodification, in sum, makes people happier.

As a word, "decommodification" may lack the allure of freedom, justice, or democracy. As we have had ample occasion to see, however, it is the single most important determinant of the general level of human happiness across, at least, the Western world. To the extent that we actually care about building a world in which more people lead lives that are more satisfying, it is clear how to proceed: protect and extend decommodification as a fundamental social priority. It is as simple as that.

Intelligent people are naturally suspicious of easy answers to what seem very complicated issues, but sometimes such answers exist, often because the question is really not that complicated. Those who benefit from the existing system of privilege—from the results of commodification—will naturally attempt to deny or obfuscate the reality that decommodification improves people's lives. Privilege always has as its first goal the perpetuation of privilege. To the extent that decommodifying institutions succeed, they do so because they limit commodification, which is to say they limit the institutional basis of privilege. We should not expect the Right to accept the results of research on happiness any more than they accept the research on climate change. They remain wrong all the same.

Chapter 4

Consumption, the Economy and Happiness

A bumper sticker from the 1980s proclaims: "He who dies with the most toys wins." Whether or not it is intended to be ironic, and "he" refers to all people or only to males, the statement reflects a widely-shared perception that happiness and success come from having more income, consuming more, and possessing more material objects. How well a person is doing is popularly interpreted to refer to a person's income and material possessions, and good jobs are seen as those which yield high income. The sentiment is also reflected in a central postulate of mainstream neoclassical economics, that is, the utility obtained by people (which they aim to maximize) depends mainly on their consumption and income and that, loosely speaking, people prefer having more to having less. Utility, of course, can depend on many other things. For instance, in examining the labor-leisure choice, it is taken to depend on leisure. It may also depend on saving, but that is so because it makes future consumption possible. In most applications consumption and income are seen as the major determinants. Even the (socially desirable) efficiency of the economy is usually perceived in terms of the amount of goods and services available.

But does money really buy happiness? The view that it does has found many dissenters, among, for instance, moral philosophers and religious traditions, who —as discussed earlier— have drawn attention to the problem that the pursuit of income and consumption has diverted people's attention from more important goals that bring "true" happiness, and from those who are concerned with the negative effects of continued increases in income and consumption on the community, public life, and the natural environment. However, the view has also been argued to be at variance with a large amount of data on the relationship between people's self-reported happiness and life satisfaction and their income and consumption.

The Empirics of Consumption, Income and Happiness

The pioneering contributions of Easterlin (1973, 2001) and others (see Frey and Stutzer, 2002), suggest a number of empirical regularities.

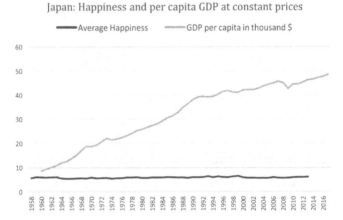

9. Happiness and real GDP per capita in Japan
Source: World Database of Happiness

Time series data for individual countries (such as the U.S. and Japan, with high levels of per capita income) do not reflect significant (and, in some cases, any) increases in the average level of self-reported happiness over time, despite significant increases in income and consumption. Graphic 9 shows the data for Japan where, despite significant changes in income and production per capita (including some reductions), average happiness changed very little. The case of the U.S. is very similar although, unlike in Japan, the level of happiness has fluctuated more. Long time-series data for lower-income countries are not available, but their experience turns out to be not very different from that of high-income countries. The case of India is shown in Graphic 10, in which average happiness figures are available for only a few years prior to 2006, but the more recent happiness data shows that average happiness has been going down despite significant increases in per capita real production and income!

10. **Happiness and real GDP per capita in India**
Source: World Database of Happiness

Panel data on specific groups of individuals over their lives suggest that despite increases in income, these individuals do not experience significant increases in self-reported happiness. Cross-sectional data across countries suggest that although, on average, countries with higher levels of per capita income and consumption do have higher average levels of self-reported happiness, beyond a certain level of income (just below the threshold of what is normally thought of as defining high income countries), there is no positive relationship. This can be seen in Graphic 11, which shows happiness score averages for 2014-16 taken from the World Happiness Report of 2017, and real per capita GDP (using purchasing power parity (PPP) figures to take into account price differences across countries) averages for 2014-16, with each diamond representing a different country. Even individuals who win lotteries have been found to report no greater happiness after a few years. In terms of more objective measures of happiness, there is even some evidence to suggest that lifetime risk of mental disorders increases with per capita income across countries (Hidaka, 2012), although some of this can be explained by different rates of diagnosis.

HAPPINESS SCORE (VERTICAL AXIS)
PER CAPITA GDP IN US$ PPP (HORIZONTAL AXIS), 2014-16

11. GDP per capita and Happiness in the U.S. between 2014 and 2016
Source: World Happiness Report, 2017

To be sure, there is some support for the income/ consumption-happiness connection. Cross-sectional evidence within countries seems consistent with it: people in higher income groups with higher levels of consumption report higher levels of self-reported happiness than people in lower income groups. This is shown in Figure 12 for the U.S. case, which shows that a higher percentage of people report being very happy or pretty happy (as opposed to not too happy) as their household income increases; it seems that it is better to be richer than poorer in a particular society at a particular point in time. Cross-country studies do suggest a positive income-happiness link at low levels of income. Some recent cross-country analysis even suggests that happiness actually rises with income (Stevenson and Wolfers, 2008). Some studies suggest that people are happier—even if temporarily—if their consumption and income increases.

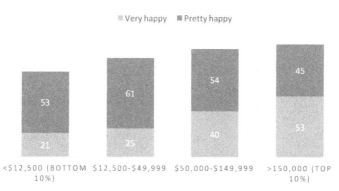

Percentage very happy and pretty happy in the U.S. by income groups, 2006

Very happy   Pretty happy

53	61	54	45
21	25	40	53
<$12,500 (BOTTOM 10%)	$12,500-$49,999	$50,000-$149,999	>150,000 (TOP 10%)

12. Percentage of happiness at different income levels for U.S. households
Source: General Social Survey data

However, the bulk of the evidence seems to contradict the consumption-happiness relationship. This is also suggested by some other measures of happiness and related evidence. Kahneman and Deaton (2010), for instance, find that increases in income improve cognitive evaluations of life, but do not improve *emotional* well-being (as measured, for example, by average levels of worry, sadness, and stress). For more objective measures, there even seems to be a negative relationship across countries between lifetime risk of mood disorders and per capita GDP (Hidaka, 2012). Although this may represent underreporting in some lower-income countries, the fact that some low-income countries have high levels of disorders and some high-income countries have low levels seems to suggest that there is some validity to the general lack of a positive relationship between income and happiness, a finding that has been called the Easterlin paradox, after the pioneering scholar mentioned earlier.

Why Increasing Consumption and Income may not Increase Happiness

To see why increasing consumption and income may not increase happiness, it is useful to ask why people seek higher levels of income. They do this for a number of reasons. First, to increase their consumption now and in the future, which they believe makes them happier. Second, to feel more financially secure. Third, to compete with others, or to gain status. Finally, to become more powerful, to be able to influence other people and society in ways that they perceive to be in their advantage: power and plenty (of money) have long been known to be related to each other. While the fourth reason may apply mainly to the very rich, the other three are likely to relate to most people.

When people's income increases, their consumption also increases, as shown by the well-known concept of the consumption function. But why does people's happiness not increase significantly over time and across countries when their income and consumption increases? Several mechanisms can be used to explain not only why many people increase their consumption when they are able to, but also—more importantly for our purposes—why increases in consumption, and income, may not significantly increase happiness, as judged by the consumers themselves (see Dutt, 2009, on which the following discussion draws). A general reason, emphasized by Easterlin (2001) is that as people consume more and have higher levels of income, they tend to increase their aspirations, which makes them less happy at a particular level of income when aspirations increase. But this explanation, by itself, does not explain why aspirations increase and why they increase just enough to offset the effects of income gains.

Needs-based Explanation

A needs-based explanation starts from the observation that the amount of real income required to satisfy a given level of needs has increased over time. This observation explains both why consumption increases and why these increases have not made people better off. People who are used to meeting a given level of needs have to consume more goods and services to meet those needs. But since the same level of needs is being satisfied, people are no better off. It has been argued that, at least in the United States, although consumption has increased significantly, the amount of income required to satisfy fundamental economic needs (for such things as safe housing, education, transportation and food) has also increased significantly, so that people are not really better off: they are merely consuming more to satisfy the same needs that they earlier satisfied with less goods.

While this explanation seems plausible enough, it is not clear that increases in the consumption of a large range of goods only reflects the reduced ability of goods to fulfill the same needs, and that they do not imply that more needs are being fulfilled. For instance, the argument that the need-required income for housing has grown considerably because real house prices (for the median sales price of existing homes) have increased, and because of the decline in personal safety, which has increased the need for safe and more expensive housing, does not take into account that the quality of (median price) houses may have improved as well, implying that the more expensive houses are satisfying additional needs and thereby increasing happiness. Moreover, it is not clear from the explanation why the efficiency of goods in satisfying needs has fallen in such a way that consumption improvements just satisfy the same needs.

Psychological Explanations

The psychological literature has drawn attention to the roles of habit formation and adaptation, and even to addiction. The essential idea is that people get used to the state they are in, and that changes in, rather than levels of, relevant states produce positive effects on their happiness. Regarding consumption, happiness depends more on increases in the level of consumption, rather than on the level of consumption. This implies that people will seek to increase consumption to increase their happiness, but once they have done so, and attained a higher level of consumption, their level of happiness will be no higher unless they continue to increase their level of consumption. Within economics, several contributions, including those by Scitovsky (1976), who examines the contradictions between comfort and stimulation, and Frank (1999) have discussed this issue and analyzed its implications. Addiction is an extreme example of this: addiction makes people want to consume increasingly larger amounts of addictive things (which can go well beyond those goods which involve chemicals, such as recreational drugs) to get further increases in satisfaction, but this leads to undesirable effects on their well-being and overall happiness.

Consumption and Time

The fact that consumption takes time directly (since it takes time to consume many things) and indirectly (it takes time to work and earn income to buy consumption goods and services) can imply that increases in consumption can occur without increases in happiness. Since consumption takes time and because, arguably, time is the ultimate scarce resource, increases in the purchase of consumer goods need not increase consumers' happiness because consumers do not have the time required to actually consume them. Moreover, increases in the time required for work to earn income, and for consumption, reduces the time people can spend on other things which can increase their happiness, such as time spent with friends and family, in doing physical activities, indulging in hobbies which provide "flow," and in sleeping, which includes an afternoon siesta. In addition, the urge to increase income and consumption can induce people to choose jobs that pay the most, without taking into account other considerations that can make people happy at work.

Although these arguments seem plausible enough, further reflection suggests that they are open to some criticisms. First, although in many cases consumption does take time, there are many kinds of consumption that take very little, or no, time at all. We can wear clothes and jewelry without allocating time to their consumption. Things—like a large house or expensive cars—consumed for status reasons are only for show and do not take time for enjoyment (although they may involve more time for cleaning and maintenance). Second, some consumer goods and services (such as household equipment like washing and drying machines, faster travel and faster communications through email) may appear to save time, but there is little evidence that they actually do so, because people insist on higher standards of cleanliness and because they travel and communicate more. Third, if people do need time to consume, why do they not take the time constraint into account in deciding how much to buy and consume? While it is possible that people sometimes do not realize that they have a time constraint when they buy things (perhaps because they are myopic about the future) and do not take into account the opportunity cost of time in the same way as they take into account actual monetary costs (as suggested by behavioral economists), these arguments are unlikely to appeal to those economists who rigidly adhere to the notion of the optimizing agent.

Sales Promotion Activities

Increases in consumption have often been explained in terms of the sales-promotion activities of firms and the media. Galbraith (1958) argues that wants increase as production increases, in large part because as production increases firms try to sell more, produce new goods, and spend more on sales promotion. Thus, firms are not necessarily responding to "wants," but are actually creating them through their own efforts, and Galbraith argues that since these are artificially-created wants, their satisfaction does not really make consumers better off.

Such arguments concerning the role of sales promotion in increasing consumption and in explaining why such increases may not increase happiness have been severely criticized by several writers. Some have argued that there is no evidence that increases in total advertising expenditure increases total consumption (although it may shift purchases from one firm to another). Others argue that consumers are not mere pawns in the hands of firms and the media, and have the final say on what they buy. Moreover, even if external influences such as sales promotions influence what and how much people buy, it does not follow that people are not made better off by such purchases. These criticisms, however, do not hold water: the empirical research does not take a sufficiently broad view of sales promotion expenditures, the argument about the ability of sales promotion activity to influence consumer decisions overlooks a great deal of behavioral economics evidence and theory, and the absence of a relationship between consumption and happiness over time seems to vindicate Galbraith's position about the effects of increasing consumption on happiness.

Borrowing and Consumer Debt

Consumer borrowing and debt can explain both increases in consumption and why consumers do not become happier by consuming more. Increases in consumption are explained by the fact that consumers have easier access to credit, something that has occurred not only in rich countries like the U.S. but also in less-developed countries, and something that is reflected in a strong upward trend in consumer debt-GDP ratios in many countries. As people obtain more credit and consume more, however, their debt level increases. This tendency has been shown to increase when people use credit cards (which seem less constraining than handing over cash) and buy things online (when impulse buying becomes easier). Increases in debt reduce happiness, as is suggested by Brown, Taylor and Price (2005) who use British Household Panel data to show that levels of outstanding debt other than home mortgage debt have a significantly negative effect on happiness, controlling for other variables such as family income, age and other personal characteristics, savings and expected changes in financial conditions.

This explanation, however, is open to some criticisms. First, it can be asked why, when credit is offered, people willingly borrow to increase their consumption. In other words, why do individuals increase their consumption to an extent that they are worse off because of increases in debt? Second, it is sometimes argued that high levels of indebtedness and consequent bankruptcy are primarily due to unexpected events like medical expenses from health problems, unemployment and divorce. But one can still ask: why do consumers not save enough to protect themselves against such contingencies? Third, although the number of people with high levels of debt and running into financial problems is increasing, those with such problems do not seem to be large enough to explain the non-increasing levels of happiness.

Consuming because Others Consume

The recent literature on why people consume suggests that an important reason why consumers buy more is that other consumers buy more (see, for instance, Hirsch, 1978, Schor, 1998, Frank, 1999, and Layard, 2005). This happens for a number of reasons.

First, individuals are seen as deriving—or perceiving that they derive—benefits in terms of higher levels of income by consuming more than others with whom they are competing. Examples include spending more on clothing than others to make a good impression on prospective employers and clients, spending more on education to become more attractive to potential employers, and consuming more in general to attract more desirable mates who will help them to increase their absolute levels of income and consumption (Frank, 1999). This motive for increasing consumption can be called the instrumental motive because relative consumption is not valued for its own sake but for its effect on absolute consumption.

Second, the nature of certain goods that makes the happiness derived from them dependent on what others consume. Following Hirsch (1976), we can call them positional goods. For instance, if what one wishes to consume is a good view of nature (say, the seashore), then the height of one's house or apartment and its distance from the seashore are relevant, but what is important is not so much the absolute height of one's house and the distance from the seashore but what these are in comparison to the houses owned by others. Hirsch (1976) has argued that goods are very likely to have such positional properties if their supply is very limited.

Third, the acquisition of goods by others serves as a form of publicity for the goods, and may make us want to increase our consumption of them because of the information we obtain about them. Or, we may think that something is of high quality simply because others have bought it. In some cases, more information can lead us to be happier when goods are purchased, but if seeing other consume results in impulse purchases it can cause unhappiness. Moreover, it is not necessarily the case that other people are benefiting from their consumption and, even if they are, that the emulator will also benefit.

A fourth involves network externalities. If many people in society have telephones, answering machines, fax machines or e-mail, not having them excludes us from the flow of information or from other experiences we value and reduces our level of happiness. In cases where these networks affect one's income (for instance, failure to make a sale or obtain a job interview), this is equivalent to the instrumental motive. In other cases, in which people's happiness directly depends on these externalities (for example, by being in contact with one's friends), we see that relative consumption matters directly as well. The notion of network externalities can be extended to goods such as books and music, if their consumption allows discussions with others and the ability to make friends.

A fifth relates to consumption norms. If most people consume something, a consumption norm is created which makes individuals "need" to consume it. Adam Smith (1776, p. 351-2)) wrote about this more than two centuries ago:

By necessaries I understand not only the commodities which are indispensably necessary for the support of life, but what ever the custom of the country renders it indecent for creditable people, even the lowest order to be without ... Custom ... has rendered leather shoes a necessary of life in England. The poorest creditable person of either sex would be ashamed to appear in public without them.

The need being fulfilled here, according to Sen (1999), is the need of not being ashamed; Smith is clearly arguing that the commodity capable of satisfying this need depends on what many others do, and is therefore changeable as customs change. In our times, if most people have straight teeth, it is likely to make the rest be ashamed to have crooked teeth, so that parents obtain braces for their children to avoid shame. Although consumption norms are likely to be strongest for goods visible to others, they may apply to other goods as well, because not consuming them can damage one's self-respect.

A final explanation is status. If we define status as the position one has in society as perceived by others on a scale of income or wealth, that individuals prefer a higher status than a lower status, and that income or wealth are not directly observable but consumption (at least of some kinds) is, individuals will try to consume more to improve their status. Although the importance of status and conspicuous consumption has been pointed out by several writers in the last three centuries or so, it has not been absorbed into mainstream economic theory and given its due. Its importance was recognized by John Rae, to some extent by Smith, and by Nassau Senior, but then de-emphasized by neoclassical economists. Veblen (1899) emphasized that individuals seek to gain status through the conspicuous consumption of leisure and, more importantly, of goods. Until very recently, however, these contributions have not had much impact on mainstream economics, and status consumption has been studied more by other social scientists such as sociologists and anthropologists, and by marketing researchers. Recent work by economists has paid more attention to the status issue, both in the theoretical and empirical literature (see, for instance, Schor, 1998, and Frank, 1999).

It may be noted that all six of these explanations can account for why people consume more when others do and for why people's happiness depends on how their relative consumption affects their utility. The information and network externality explanations are consistent with the idea that absolute levels of consumption increase happiness significantly, but the other arguments are likely to imply that absolute increases in consumption do not significantly increase happiness: for instance, if consumption increases to increase status or maintain one's self respect, increases in average consumption are likely to completely nullify the positive effects of increases in one's own consumption.

The Relative Importance of the Explanations

Three comments on the relative importance of these explanations are in order. One, individuals may consume specific goods for a number of the reasons discussed above, which may reinforce each other. Thus, even if a professional buys more expensive clothing for the instrumental reason, he or she may be doing it partly for the status or social-norms motives. This implies that the latter two motives may be more prevalent than is sometimes believed. Two, some of the explanations apply to particular goods, whereas the norms and, especially, the status explanations apply to a broad range of goods. Thus, network externalities, instrumental reasons, intrinsically positional properties, and information issues may be important for specific goods. It is, however, not appropriate to identify the status-conferring value of one isolated good; status-motivated consumption is more accurately identified by a whole range of products. Indeed, it is impossible to determine the meaning or value of goods in post-modern societies by taking each good individually, since goods reveal their purpose only when they are considered together. This meaning is particularly important for status-related consumption. This implies that consumption norms and status consumption explanations are likely to be much more important empirically than the other explanations.

Three, the relative consumption hypothesis can explain or complement some of the alternative explanations mentioned earlier. A plausible explanation of why more income is needed to satisfy the same level of needs can be found in the relative consumption hypothesis. We have already discussed how, for instance in the case of footwear, what is required to satisfy the need not to be ashamed may depend on what others consume. Sometimes consumption needs may not just reflect psychological processes, but may translate into the non-availability or inferiority of less expensive substitutes and therefore create the necessity of spending more to meet virtually the same needs. As more people use private cars as means of transportation the support for public transportation may diminish, public transportation services may decline or even diminish, requiring other people to buy cars as well. As more people consume expensive goods cheaper substitutes may not be produced if the market for them is not large enough to make them profitable to cover costs in the presence of fixed costs or increasing returns to scale. As more people use refrigeration, small nearby groceries for daily shopping may vanish, requiring others to shop less frequently at distant supermarkets and buy refrigerators. As people buy bigger cars, it can become less safe to drive in smaller cars, requiring small-car owners to buy bigger and more expensive cars. In all these cases, increases in consumption by others induce people to consume more. But all this is one variant of our relative consumption hypothesis.

Regarding the psychological explanations, there

is some relation between them and our relative consumption hypothesis. First, habit formation may partly reflect internal adaptation, but is also likely to have a social aspect, that is, people may get used to things not just because they consume it, but also because others do, and this may become embodied in social norms. Second, as Scitovsky (1976) notes, not all consumer goods lead to boredom. Some goods, as Frank (1999) argues, lead to gains that last. If people buy and seek novelty in goods that they see others consuming, and not goods that they can spend many hours and years enjoying, they are more likely to get bored with them. Thus, consuming goods because others consume them is likely to lead people to get more adapted to them, preventing them from buying goods which provide lasting gains.

On the time constraint argument, a plausible explanation for the emergence of time constraints is that consumers value their relative consumption in addition to their absolute level of consumption which, as discussed earlier, leads to working too much and having too little leisure. This also makes them switch increasingly to consumption goods which do not take much time to consume, a substitution effect brought about by the shortage of time. Moreover, having less time to spend on obtaining information about goods, consumers may rely more on observing what others are consuming in judging their desirability. All this increases the importance of relative consumption.

On sales promotion, although, in principle, the activities of firms can have an effect on consumer behavior by increasing their aspirations in a manner unrelated to the relative consumption hypothesis, sales promotion activities of firms and the relative consumption hypothesis—keeping up with the Joneses, for instance—are related. First, advertisements, television shows and films extend the reference groups of consumers, making them want to consume what other people do, including celebrities and imagined people with whom they would not otherwise come into contact. Second, advertisers often work on consumers in complicated ways that exploit their propensity to emulate and seek status by suggesting—in subtle and sometimes not-so-subtle ways—why this or that product will increase their status or make them more like people who are rich and beautiful. Thus, firms and the media may have an important role in ensuring the relevance of the relative consumption effect.

Finally, on the consumer debt argument: people desire to consume more even though it does not increase their happiness, and do not save enough for precautionary purposes, because they are induced to do so because their happiness depends on relative consumption. Of course, cuts in government programs on health care which imply more out-of-pocket expenses can also increase indebtedness, so that relative consumption is not the only thing at work.

If not Consumption, then what Economic Factors affect Happiness?

If consumption and income do not significantly affect happiness, at least beyond a certain level of income, one may ask if there are any economic factors that do affect it. Happiness in a variety of senses has been found to be affected by a variety of factors, and some of these are what may be called "economic" ones in a fairly narrow sense (see Frey and Stutzer, 2002).

Something that has been consistently found to have a negative effect on measures such as subjective well-being and life satisfaction is unemployment, not only for individuals who are unemployed, but also for society as a whole. For individuals, being unemployed leads to a loss of income, but the effect of unemployment is negative when income is controlled for; that is, for instance, when income is maintained by unemployment benefits. This can happen because of the loss of self-esteem, self-confidence, and conflict within the family (that sometimes leads to divorce), and studies of the mental health effects of unemployment confirm these effects. It does not seem that most people who are unemployed enjoy their "vacations" and "living on the dole." Overall happiness in a country is affected negatively by the unemployment rate in that country (keeping other things constant) if unemployed people are less happy than those who are employed. However, there are some additional reasons why this aggregate unemployment rate may negatively affect happiness, because even those who are employed may become more insecure of job loss and the possibility of finding another job if unemployment is high, and even sympathize with those who are unemployed.

In addition to unemployment, inflation is a macroeconomic indicator that attracts widespread attention. Economists generally argue that, with other things like real income unchanged, people are not made worse off by moderate rates of inflation, if their income in money terms increases proportionately with prices, apart from some minor costs, for instance, if they hold currency and other assets denominated in money terms, and the "menu" costs resulting from price changes. However, they are concerned with higher rates of inflation because of the fact that different prices rise at different rates in an uncertain manner. This increase in uncertainty makes people less happy, but also it results in inefficiencies by not allowing markets to allocate resources efficiently because prices show "noise" rather than real scarcities and surpluses. Studies across time and across countries typically suggest that higher rates of inflation imply lower levels of subjective well-being. But this may have less to do with the small costs that economists emphasize, and more to do with the fact that different people may be affected differently by inflation (for instance, creditors may be affected adversely but not debtors, and people with relatively fixed money incomes), and by the fact that people keep mental and written accounts in money terms, and perceive themselves to be worse off with inflation because they experience increasing prices of goods and services they buy (even when their money income rises, which they may attribute to their own merit). Many economists and monetary authorities pay more attention to reducing inflation (following what is called inflation targeting) than to reducing unemployment (which they believe would be inflationary). Empirical studies, however, show people are more strongly affected by increases in unemployment than by similar increases in inflation.

The rate of economic growth has also been found to have a positive effect on subjective well-being, holding other things constant. This may be because people feel better off when income and consumption is increasing, as noted earlier. However, as discussed earlier, these gains may be short-lived unless the economy continues growing at a high rate.

It has sometimes been found that an increase in income inequality has a negative effect on measures of subjective well-being, other things held constant. This seems to be true for some countries but not for all, with the U.S. being one where the data does not show this negative effect (Senik, 2005). There could be a number of reasons why this may occur. One has to do with what is called diminishing marginal utility, that is, the additional utility or happiness derived from additional amounts of income decrease when income increases. This implies that if, starting from a position in which two people get the same level of income, so that there is equality of income, the income of one person is increased and that of the other is reduced by the same amount, so that average income remains the same but inequality increases, average utility will fall, since the gain in utility experienced by the person who has become rich will be smaller than the loss in utility experienced by the person who has become poor. This argument can be generalized to the case of many people and to situations in which we do not start with complete equality. In addition, differences in how happiness depends on the relative income of low- and high-income people can have a role. The happiness of people with lower levels of income is likely to depend on the absolute level of their income and also on their income relative to people who have higher levels of income. However, the happiness of people with higher levels of income is likely to depend mainly on their income relative to those of other high-income people (and not on the income of low income people) and not on their absolute level of income, since most of their needs have already been satisfied. If this is case, an increase in inequality will reduce the happiness of low income people much more (because of the reduction in their absolute income and the fall in their income relative to that of the rich) than it will raise the happiness of high income people (since their happiness does not depend on their absolute income or their income relative to the poor), and thereby reduce overall happiness. In some countries, such as the U.S., this inequality-happiness relationship may not hold, because more inequality may make lower income people believe that they have the chance to move up and increase their income significantly. As it turns out, however, perceptions of economic mobility in the U.S. are lower than actual mobility.

In addition to not being unemployed, the happiness of people has been found to depend on the kind of work people do. Warr (1999) finds that people are made happier by the intrinsic aspects of their work—such as their sense of autonomy and independence, and the meaning they attach to their work—rather than by their extrinsic aspects, such as the income they receive from it.

Finally, economic security can be expected to make people happier. Increases in the level of income at low levels of income are likely to make a larger contribution to the sense of economic security than at higher levels of income. Moreover, as argued extensively in the previous chapter, decommodification and stronger social safety nets have the same effect.

Consumption, Income and the Socio-economic System

Increases in consumption and income may not increase happiness for the individuals who experience such increases, at least beyond a point. But it may be argued that such increases in aggregate consumption can have a positive effect on overall happiness by affecting other things at the systemic level that are affected by such increases. To take one example, increases in consumption can increase aggregate demand, output and employment, and thereby reduce unemployment which, as we saw earlier, increases happiness.

President George W. Bush asked people in the United States, two weeks after the September 11, 2001, terrorist attacks, to spend more to help the country. "Get down to Disney World in Florida," he advised, "[t]ake your families and enjoy life, the way we want it to be enjoyed," to increase consumption spending, including that on air travel, and prevent an economic downturn. Many economists argue that even if increases in consumer spending can reduce unemployment in the short run, it will not do so in the medium and longer run, because the economy will be more or less at full employment (or at the non-accelerating inflation rate of unemployment or NAIRU), so that it will only reduce saving and, as a result, investment and economic growth. But it can be pointed out that aggregate demand may affect output and unemployment over long periods of time if unemployment is persistent, and if the NAIRU changes over time due to changes in aggregate demand, as some empirical evidence suggests. Increases in consumption, as we have seen earlier, can be financed by consumer borrowing and have the result of increasing consumer debt. This, over time, is likely to increase income inequality because it will transfer income from lower income borrowers to higher income lenders, which will eventually depress consumption demand (because low income groups tend to consume a higher percentage of their income than high income groups) as debt burdens increase. If aggregate demand is to be increased to reduce unemployment, there may be better ways of doing so—by directly reducing income inequality and by increasing government spending by raising taxes.

There are several additional reasons why increases in total consumption and the factors that make it increase can have other effects on society at the aggregate level that can adversely affect happiness. The urge to increase individual consumption is likely to add to the reasons (such as distrust for the government) why people may vote for lower taxes and lower government spending. If people want to increase their own levels of private consumption, they are less likely to want to pay taxes that will reduce their ability to spend more on themselves, and less likely to support spending on goods that economists call public goods, which can be enjoyed by all and from which people cannot be excluded if they do not pay for it. These include roads, food and drug regulation, environmental regulation and the like, which can affect people's happiness. There will also be less support for redistributive fiscal policy and the security provided by social safety nets, also reducing happiness.

Increases in consumption and the forces that drive it also make people: seek employment in work that pays more than work they enjoy intrinsically; work longer hours, and move to places where they can obtain higher wages, having less time for developing friendships and family relationships; and, in effect, damage the environment more directly due to their consumption and indirectly by allowing firms to produce and sell more. We have discussed some of these issues already, and will return to the last two issues in the next chapter.

Chapter 5

The Environments Shaping Happiness

The two previous chapters focused on the political and economic foundations of happiness. We turn here to the other major set of influences on happiness: the social environment and the natural environment. Simply put, we live in a set of nested contexts, which is convenient to think of as the environment of our lives. The most obvious of these is the quality of the natural world around us—our ecosystem, and the human effect upon it, as manifest in pollution, climate change, and the generalized neglect of the planet. The other, which we examine first, is the social or human environment—the quality of human interactions, relative to those that best promote happiness.

The Social Environment

The social environment refers to the way individuals and groups interact with each other in (largely) non-economic contexts (those that do not involve buying, selling, producing and consuming). This involves family members, friends, neighbors, as well as the myriad of other persons we interact with in other aspects of life, including those we see in institutionalized contexts—such as sports leagues and hobbyist clubs, charitable and other volunteer organizations, and political parties, to take but a few examples.

Social relationships have long been seen as a major determinant of happiness. Thus, we have already had occasion to discuss some aspects of social interactions, for instance, when individual consumers were seen to be affected by what other individuals and groups do in order to (among other things) express their identities, increase their social status, or conform to social norms. We have also had occasion to see the power of institutions, like labor unions and labor market regulations, to influence relationships among coworkers (and indirectly between workers and their families, friends, etc.). In what follows, we examine social relations in both a narrower (family relationships, friendship, etc.) and a wider sense (conceptions of society as a whole).

Let us begin with an inexpensive observation: as the example of labor unions exemplifies, economic and political factors affect many aspects of the social environment. In particular, it is widely agreed that when people are driven by materialistic goals, such that they make decisions about their lives myopically focused on career, status and income, they are less likely to be able to form strong and fulfilling relationships with others (if for no other reason than that time and emotional energy are finite, such that more focus on one's career means less attention to family and friends, by definition). Further, while economic interactions may sometimes contribute to human connections, market relationships in general do not, in that they often have a competitive and conflictual aspect that robs them of intimacy or even sincerity. To scholars of happiness, it seems clear that, once our basic human needs are fulfilled, a rewarding life depends upon building and nurturing connections to our fellows. As Albert Einstein succinctly puts it, "Man can find happiness in this life only by devoting himself to society" (where by "society" he means connections to others).

That view is as old as human civilization. Aristotle, writing in the fourth century BCE, famously viewed friendship to be absolutely vital for human flourishing (Book 8.1): "Without friends no one would choose to live, though he had all other goods; even rich men and those in possession of office and of dominating power are thought to need friends most of all; for what is the use of such prosperity without the opportunity of beneficence, which is exercised chiefly and in its most laudable form towards friends? Or how can prosperity be guarded and preserved without friends?" Thus, neither wealth nor power obviate the need for friendship. Aristotle (Book 8.3) also recognized that true friendship—or *philia*—is not pursued for utility (so that one can obtain something of value through friendship, some use that people can get from another) or one's own pleasure, but instead must be motivated by one's care for those one calls friend. We will be closer to happiness, he argues, when we have more and better friends in this sense.

Recent empirical studies have found that having family relationships and friends are among the major determinants of emotional and cognitive well-being. Friendship, measured by whether a person has a best friend, the number of one's friends, and the quality of these friendships, have been found to have statistically significant effects on happiness indicators, controlling for other factors (see, for instance, Demir and Weitekamp, 2007). Some studies have also explored mechanisms through which friendship increases happiness, including directly fulfilling our human need for intimacy and connection, as well as indirect benefits, such as the greater economic security that friendship implies. It is also worth stressing that not all friendships are of equal value—or even that not all things we label as friendship correspond to the traditional meaning. Thus, having many "friends" on social media, with whom one does not have close interactions, may actually reduce happiness, as they may crowd out genuine "real life" relationships).

Perhaps the strongest evidence for the centrality of human connection to happiness is the vast number of studies confirming that married (or even just romantically cohabiting) people are consistently found to be happier than all others (whether single, separated, divorced, and widowed). The importance of having a life partner is evident not merely in the uniformity of the evidence for its link to happiness, but in the equal uniformity of the intensity of the connection. Study after study confirms that marriage is one (perhaps the) single most important predictor of happiness, being dramatically more important than virtually all demographic factors (with the possible exception of unemployment).

The scholarly evidence in general seems to suggest that social connections of any (non-market) kind promote happiness. The most frequently cited example is attendance of religious services. The more people attend church, in sum, the happier they are, net of other factors. While many people surely take comfort from religion itself, the empirical connection between church attendance and happiness is thought to have little or nothing to do with the explicitly religious nature of these social interactions, but instead reflects a general pattern, applicable to any non-commercial organization one voluntarily belongs to: people involved in groups of any kind (at least those that involve face-to-face meetings) tend to enjoy life more. This applies to participation in everything from amateur sports teams (or, indeed, to fans watching professional sports on television together), civic groups (e.g. neighborhood associations, parenting groups, charities, volunteers at an animal shelter), political organizations (e.g. a local chapter of Amnesty International, or the local constituency association for a political party), and so on.

Immersion in these kind of networks is central to the idea of "social capital." Briefly put, social capital refers to two related things: (a) a vibrant civil society, in which there is a proliferation of voluntary groups that many people participate in, for reasons (mostly) devoid of a commercial incentive, and (b) there exists, partially as a result, wide social acceptance of norms of trust and reciprocity. The first point stresses that participation in voluntary groups promotes human connections, which itself contributes substantially to the emotional well-being of those involved (in that such connections are part of the needs as social animals). Further, the civic education that comes from group membership—of meeting and working with others, hearing their points of view, coming to amenable collective decisions—tends to promote the pro-social attitudes summarized by the phrase "norms of trust and reciprocity." Such norms are obviously beneficial: life is easier, and better, when we normally believe that other people are, essentially, trustworthy, and when we expect that our trust in others will be reciprocated. While it takes no great insight to believe that people will be happier in societies where such norms are prevalent, the empirical research confirms this contention. Simply put, greater social capital implies greater human well-being.

The discussion above, following the mainstream literature on happiness and social capital, depends upon the conceptualization of social capital popularized by the American political scientist Robert Putnam (2000). While Putnam's work has been hugely influential, it stands in opposition to the equally venerable and compelling treatment of social capital exemplified by the French sociologist Pierre Bourdieu (1986). Bourdieu embeds and defines his notion of social capital within a richly generalized theory of society and power that does not lend itself to brief or ready explanation. In brief, Bourdieu focuses on how social classes use different and interacting forms of capital, including social capital, to form and reproduce themselves in relation to each other to attempt to advance their own position, which has implications for privilege, oppression and resistance. He criticizes the Putnam-style of analysis on several grounds, the most important of which depends ultimately on his rejection of the idea, implicit in Putnam, that voluntary organizations (say, charities) reflect universalistic values, i.e. those that transcend the economic interests of those involved. Bourdieu denies that in practice such values exist—universal values are always particular values in disguise (and often invisible even to those directly involved). Without digressing too much into the theoretical quicksand these ideas invite, the implication is that a central premise of Putnam—that actors are behaving disinterestedly in the voluntary associations at the core of this theory—may be problematic, particularly as it relates to the total net effects across all parts of the social and economic system. Thus, it could well be that volunteering does increase the amount of social welfare (both directly and secondarily through fostering interpersonal trust), but at the same time it could also reduce the total, net production of human well-being because high levels of volunteerism provide a rationale for reducing the size and generosity of the welfare state (as its functions are being absorbed by private volunteerism). In Bourdieu's terms, we would in this way have the perverse outcome of well-intentioned volunteerism serving to reinforce and protect the system of domination that class theorists stress. Given the strong connection between decommodification and human happiness, fostering social capital could in this way produce, in the end, less rather than more net well-being. Limitations of space prohibit unpacking these ideas to the degree they deserve, but one last point warrants mention: Bourdieu conceives of these kinds of transactions— volunteerism in exchange for a reduction in the size of the state—as taking place structurally, with individuals unconscious of the exchange both are complicit in making.

What this means for happiness is unclear. As noted, we do have strong evidence that social capital is correlated with greater satisfaction with life, controlling for other factors. The last phrase, though, opens the door to Bourdieu's critique: if we hold everything else constant, social capital likely does indeed improve quality of life, but this ignores the question of whether social capital is also indirectly affecting the world in negative ways, as exemplified by a reduction in the welfare state or an increase in the hegemony of the neo-liberal ideology that is evidently hostile to an agenda of the greatest happiness for the greatest number.

The Natural Environment

The natural environment, often referred to as the environment, encompasses all living and non-living things that exist naturally (that is, not constructed by humans) on the earth or some part of it, and includes such things as the quantity and quality of water, air quality, forest cover and tress, soil quality, solid and hazardous waste, stocks of exhaustible resources (like minerals and oil), animal stocks, biodiversity, weather, the ozone layer and, of course, global climate.

It is widely recognized that economic expansion and increasing affluence and consumption in many parts of the world have caused environmental damage. Natural resources are either used up or damaged due to production, consumption and the expansion of humans (such as fossil fuels, the soil and forests) and adversely affected by production, transportation and consumption (due to, for instance, air and water pollution). Many economists argue that environmental damage does not necessarily increase as per capita income increases in a country, and the problem is already being mitigated in some places. This is shown by what is called the environmental Kuznets curve, which shows that although environmental indicators initially get worse when income per person increases, it eventually gets better. This is argued to happen because of several reasons. First, as the stock of some natural resources, called exhaustible resources, get depleted, such as oil and other fossil fuels for which fixed supplies exist (at least for the relevant time horizon), their prices will tend to increase, which will stimulate the development of technology involving other forms of energy that will reduce dependence on these fuels. In other words, the market mechanism will take care of the problem. Second, as countries become richer and attain what is called their post-industrial stage, the consumption of industrial goods will fall in relative terms, being replaced by less environmentally damaging service consumption (such as that of the fine arts).

These solutions, however, may not be enough, since people will still need to consume goods and services such as transportation, which will continue to damage the environment because of what economists call externalities, that is, the damage production and consumption by firms and people causes and which adversely harms other people, who are not compensated by the consumers and producers who therefore have no incentive to reduce the damage. For instance, when people buy cars, they pay the seller and producer of cars, but the production, use and ultimate disposal of these cars results in various kinds of environment damage, including pollution while driving and during production, which harms people who breathe polluted air. This not only dirties the air near factories and cities, but also adds to greenhouse gases in the global atmosphere, which results in global warming and climate change, which also affects weather patterns, for instance, bringing drought in some parts of the world and increasing the frequency and intensity of storms in many other parts of the world, causing enormous damage.

These externalities, however, can be overcome by a third response, that is, government regulation which directly prevents polluters or imposes costs on polluters using pollution taxes or by creating markets for tradeable pollution permits which polluters have to pay for. It is argued that as people become richer and satisfy their basic needs, and as environmental problems such as air quality become worse, people will want to clean up the environment and vote for policies that introduce the necessary regulations. This will impose costs on polluters, making them adopt cleaner methods of production, and increase the costs of goods for consumers, who will consume less.

There is many a slip between cup and lip, however. For the sake of brevity we will confine ourselves to the observation that just because people want less environmental damage, it does not follow that governments will introduce suitable policies to lessen or eliminate the damage. Policies depend largely on the power of different groups and classes, and it is possible that large corporations and those who control and own many of them may strongly oppose regulation, sometimes in the name of freedom from government "interference," and many of the less powerful may be induced to side with them because they believe they will benefit from low prices due to the rolling back of regulations, even denying scientific evidence about the dangers and causes of global climate change. Even if regulations are adopted and implemented in some parts of the world, the production of goods can be moved to other countries from which they can be imported, often low-income countries, where regulation is weaker, "outsourcing" the problem, not reducing global warming even if it reduces local pollution. Indeed, the EKC has been found for some kinds of environmental damage, but not others, such as global greenhouse gas emissions.

Turning to the effects of the natural environment on happiness, we may start by noting that human beings have a long history of living in nature, in caves, forests and grasslands, where they have lived as hunters, gatherers, domesticators of animals and tillers of the soil. Living and doing well in the natural environment has arguably genetically hardwired humans into having a close psychological bond with their natural environment due to the process of evolution. Wilson (1984) has used the term "biophilia" to refer to the rich, mostly innate, pleasure that comes from being surrounded by living organisms.

Some evidence regarding subjective well-being corroborates this hypothesis. Ferrer-i-Carbonell and Gowdy (2007), using data from the British Household Panel Survey, show that concern about ozone pollution has a negative effect and concern about animal extinction has a positive effect on an individual's life satisfaction, controlling for a variety of socio-economic variables such as employment status, education and family status, and various psychological traits. They interpret these results to suggest that concerns with environmental degradation (ozone pollution in their study) has a negative effect on well-being while concern with biodiversity loss indicates a psychological bond with the living world. To examine whether or not these concerns merely reflect the actual environmental conditions people face, they control for whether individuals live in a more polluted environment and whether they engage in outdoor activities, to show that the results of environmental attitudes continue to hold and, moreover, pollution reduces and working outdoors increases life satisfaction. Thus, not only does concern with the environment make people feel better, but environmental factors, independently of these concerns, affect subjective well-being.

Turning to the effects of environmental changes, a number of studies show that indicators of happiness have been found to be affected by measures of environmental conditions. Welsch (2006) uses pooled cross-country data from ten European countries to examine how life-satisfaction is affected by different measures of pollution, that is, nitrogen dioxide and lead concentrations in the air, controlling for per capita income, using a fixed-effects econometric model to show statistically significant and strong negative effects. Taking into account the positive effect of income on life satisfaction shown by the estimates, the study shows that people are willing to give up between 16.6 and 2.3 percent of their income to reduce the actual declines in the levels of these pollutants between 1991 and 1997, depending on the country and type of pollution. Other studies have found similar results for other countries and other measures of the environment. Whatever one thinks about the monetary valuation of the environment, these studies all show that environmental problems reduce subjective well-being. The availability of green spaces in cities has also been found to affect subjective well-being.

The effects of global climate change can be assessed by using studies that examine the effects of climate and of weather-related natural disasters on subjective well-being. On climate, Rehdanz and Maddison (2005) use panel data from 67 countries to show that climate variables (such as average and peak temperatures and rainfall) have a strong and statistically significant effect on self-reported levels of happiness, controlling for other factors. The results imply that only a few high-latitude countries will experience increases in happiness due to limited increases in temperature, while low-latitude, warmer countries would experience declines. Climate-related natural disasters have also been found to reduce subjective well-being, especially in low-income countries in which people have less protection against the adverse effects of storms.

This quantitative research shows how indicators of subjective well-being and life satisfaction are affected by the environment. However, nature also affects happiness in other senses, whether in terms of pleasure and instantaneous thrills from trekking and biking in wooded areas, canoeing, fishing and surfing in rivers, lakes and oceans, skiing on snow, and rock and mountaineering, or enjoying the serenity of forests and experiencing flow by forgetting oneself and losing track of time. The aesthetic dimension of nature, as emphasized by writers such as Henry David Thoreau, evokes feelings of well-being, tranquility and peace (see Lambin, 2012). Hindu ascetics found forests and mountains to be a suitable setting in which to meditate and worship, and religious texts recommended the virtue of living in forests after enjoying family life.

It is not just measures of subjective well-being or emotional states that are affected by environmental factors. A large body of psychological research shows unambiguously that proximity to nature has positive effects of mental and physical health (see Lambin, 2012). Urban dwellers, for instance, who live in depressing surroundings without natural vegetation are more likely to suffer from chronic stress and other health problems, independently of characteristics such as age and socio-economic situation. Ulrich (1984) found, comparing patients who underwent a particular surgical procedure in a suburban Pennsylvania hospital, that those who had a room with a tree view from their window left the hospital sooner, had fewer post-surgical complications, took less pain medicine, and had fewer negative evaluative comments from nurses than did those who had a wall view, controlling for factors such as age, gender and past medical history. Numerous other studies have confirmed these results, showing how exposure to nature reduces stress, mental fatigue, headaches and medical problems in general (Lambin, 2012). Interactions with the world of animals, which provide a means of maintaining a close connection with nature, also have many mental and physical health benefits, as shown by pet ownership (especially dogs and to some extent cats) and therapy dogs, as well as positive effects on subjective well-being. A number of psychological theories, consistent with the idea of biophilia, have been proposed for understanding these effects. One emphasizes the restorative powers of directed attention through involuntary and effortless actions; another with nature offering a coherent framework of grand proportions, which suggests that there is always more to discover, and yet another asserting that nature leads to perceptions of the meaning of life with a sense of belonging to the natural world (Lambin, 2012). In addition, pets provide companionship, allow emotional interaction and reduce loneliness, lead to more interactions with other human beings (with other pet-owners or those who are attracted by pets), and help with physical exercise (for instance, by taking dogs for walks).

Environmental damage also affects well-being in objective terms—by influencing functionings and capabilities, and by reducing soil fertility and water availability, which can cause serious harm to poor farmers in low- and middle-income countries. Also, through deforestation and other damage to what are called common property resources, environmental damage reduces the consumption of the poor who obtain resources from fishing and gathering.

Overall, there is considerable evidence to suggest that environmental factors have a significant effect on the happiness and well-being of people according to a variety of measures. But this evidence arguably focuses on the tip of the iceberg. The happiness people may feel in some parts of the world due to temperature increases tell us little about the complex effects of global climate change that will occur in the future due to increases in sea level, and resulting changes in the geographical incidence of infectious diseases and similar maladies. The results will adversely affect untold people, and possibly even threaten the extinction of human life itself. Nor does the happiness of people living now capture the effects on the happiness of future generations, unless they can fully understand and represent the concerns of the latter, which is most unlikely.

Chapter 6

What is to be Done?

What does the scholarly study of happiness suggest for those who want to build a happier world? At the individual level, what strategies are recommended for leading a positive and rewarding life? At the collective level, how might we modify public policies or social structures to make life as satisfying as possible—to achieve the greatest happiness for the greatest number? As citizens of an increasingly integrated world, how can we act globally in support of human well-being?

Let us begin with some caveats. We take it for granted that happiness and well-being are, for the purpose of this discussion, broadly defined so as to incorporate not only life satisfaction per se but also wider concerns such as flourishing, tranquility and self-actualization. We will also assume that happiness is worth increasing. Although some versions of happiness can be criticized as undesirable, for instance, on account of its possible inauthenticity in a world full of problems and for its possible adverse effect on artistic creativity (see Wilson, 2008), given our broader conception of happiness, these concerns need not detain us. We also do not endorse adopting a program of maximization of happiness in a formulaic or otherwise narrow sense: the world is unlikely to be improved by replacing the current idolatry of concentrating almost entirely on promoting economic growth with a new false god predicated on maximizing only (necessarily incomplete measures of) happiness. In the end, the determinants of happiness are complex and many, such that trying to increase it in a simplistic way, as John Stuart Mill argued, is likely to be self-defeating. We must also be careful to avoid policy prescriptions that might encourage political entrepreneurs to cynically use a happiness agenda—for instance, if a cut in public services does not immediately translate to a decrease in apparent happiness, governments might tout that point as proof that the cuts were not harmful, despite the evidence that lower spending might exacerbate other social pathologies (more poverty, more crime, more homelessness, etc.) whose effects are not immediately reflected in aggregate happiness data.

A second obstacle we must overcome before turning to strategies for a happier world is the objection that however desirable it might be to increase happiness, it is in fact not possible to do so. Indeed, some have argued that people have a "set point" of happiness, determined by, say, their genes or other factors thought to shape the human personality. In this interpretation, it may only be possible to temporarily change one's level of happiness by changing their circumstances, but they inevitably return to their set points as they adapt to new conditions. There are many reasons for being skeptical about these arguments, as we have had occasion to see in prior chapters. First, at best these arguments are applicable to only some notions of happiness, not all. It is difficult, for instance, to apply these arguments to ideas beyond life satisfaction— one struggles to see how we can have programmed set points for tranquility or flourishing. Second, even for life satisfaction, set points are typically argued to determine fifty percent of the variation, with the remaining fifty percent capable of being changed through changes in activities and circumstances (see Lyubomirsky, 2007). Third, genes or personality might indeed influence happiness, but these effects are themselves variable because such dispositions interact with other factors, such as activities and circumstances, offering yet another reason people with the same genes might vary dramatically in happiness, depending on other aspects of their lives.

Finally, while adaptation doubtless does occur in some circumstances, it does not do so uniformly or mechanistically to all conditions of life. Thus, while one may readily adapt to buying a nicer house in the predicted way, one may not adapt much to day-to-day humiliations, such as a bad job, in which one is not treated with dignity or respect.

This brief chapter clearly cannot be expected to provide a comprehensive discussion of all the things that can be done to increase happiness in its various forms. Nor does this chapter intend to provide a self-help guide on how to increase one's happiness and do so quickly and painlessly. While there are a large number of such self-help books and some of them contain useful advice, here we draw some conclusions from the scholarly literature reviewed in the earlier chapters rather than providing a blueprint for being happy. Our aim is the much more modest one of illustrating that the pursuit of happiness is not entirely an individualistic endeavor. You can do much to improve your life, just as you can do much to find and keep a good job. But the labor market is also beyond your control as an individual: the availability and quality of jobs depends on the macro-economy, which in turn is the result of decisions by other actors, operating at the level of the firm, the nation, and the world. Similarly, happiness is, in the aggregate, the result of action at different levels: individual, group, nation and world. We also hope to show, as this conceptualization implies, that there are many different routes to increasing happiness, on which different scholarly disciplines can shed some light (see Dutt and Radcliff, 2009).

The Individual Level

It is easiest to initiate action individually since it can be done by one person, unilaterally, without requiring other people's agreement or reciprocation. Psychologists, especially those who work on positive psychology, have emphasized the benefits of expressing gratitude, forgiveness, and kindness towards others; avoiding overthinking about what could have been and comparing oneself to others; engaging in activities that generate "flow" such as pursuing hobbies; doing physical exercises; meditating (so as to clear one's mind, or even to leave oneself behind); practicing(or consciously electing not to practice) religion; savoring joyful experiences and thinking about them; and having goals that are meaningful and, ideally, involve helping others (see, for instance, Lyubomirsky, 2007 and Ben-Shahar, 2007).

Some of these actions can involve being mindful about what one does for pleasure and for developing oneself for the long-term (perhaps keeping a rough log of time spent watching television, being with friends, helping others), and by developing positive habits, for instance, doing physical exercises, being in nature, and spending time with others (see Ben-Shahar, 2007). Some kinds of unhappiness, such as clinical depression, require expert medical attention and often the use of medication, but overmedication to overcome feelings of sadness may be problematic, which is even more true of substance abuse. In the economic sphere one can try to work fewer hours, choose jobs that one likes and not just pay the most, and to develop other interests and compete with oneself rather than with others. One can try to consume in a way that promotes health and long-term well-being, and to obtain gains which last and do not lead to boredom, or which yield benefits that are lost when other people also consume them (such as things consumed for status). Some have recommended living a simple life with few or a limited number of material possessions, and drastic downsizing, which may be rewarding to some, while others may prefer moderation. In the social sphere, friendship and other intimate connections are among the most important contributors to a rewarding life.

By contrast, arguably the single most important institution of modern life—the market economy—is not only unable to provide such things, but may actually increase unhappiness by encouraging individuals to seek the emotionally empty consumerist goals that markets reinforce. This is one of, perhaps the, most widely-accepted conclusions to be drawn from the study of happiness: the raw materials for a satisfying life are found less in careers and (once we reach a secure and comfortable level of living) money than they are in our relationships with other people. Happiness, as we have seen, is fostered by the inclusion of individuals within social networks of all kinds, ranging from the family and friends to compatriots in political or charitable causes. The wider lesson, perhaps, is that individuals may benefit by consciously shifting their internal mental calculus away from material or career goals, substituting in their place social, political or personal goals that take them outside the world of personal economic gain. More generally still, the scholarly research confirms what most of us would like to believe: our lives are richer and more rewarding to the extent we can endeavor, at least, to embrace a value system that suggests finding purpose or meaning by looking beyond oneself, and certainly beyond materialism. It is in fact not the case that "the one with the most toys wins," but rather that we "win" by considering what it is we want. To the extent we seek genuine happiness, success is most likely to be found not in what we possess or consume, but in our attachments to others and, thus, outside of the economic sphere as conventionally construed. Happiness can also be sought in spending time in nature, walking in the woods and parks, being with animals, visiting naturally beautiful places. Religion and philosophy also provide a great deal of help for understanding different notions of happiness and their relationships—so that one can reflect on them and apply them to one's life, for giving purpose to life in a way that looks beyond oneself and self-gratification, that encourages kindness and charity, and that involves prayer and meditation.

The issues discussed above are predicated upon one having control over oneself, in the way the Stoics argued. We can, indeed, modify our attitudes toward the world, in ways that are likely to make life more agreeable. The entire field of positive psychology, thus, is devoted to the idea that we can reprogram our minds to have a higher level of happiness, as well as to reduce the degree to which we adapt (i.e. take for granted) positive life events. Both are useful strategies, as is the idea noted above that we can change our internal mental processes by thoughtful reflection on the real causes of happiness—so as to be happier, say, by learning to focus on what really creates happiness and what does not.

At the same time, it is at least as important to consider the lessons learned from the research on immediate and tangible life goals and strategies. Thus, as we have observed several times, greater income contributes only modestly at best to greater happiness (once we have escaped poverty). Again, this in turn suggests pursuing career or employment strategies that provide things beyond income, in that these are not subject to the diminishing effects of social comparison that render more consumption a poor strategy for happiness. Thus, we do better when we focus on things such as the inherent value or pleasure taken in the work itself, job security, how easily a job lends itself to an agreeable work-life balance, and whether one is represented by a labor union. The literature also highlights the importance of other factors that individuals may not be able to unilaterally control but which they have the initiative in pursuing, the most important of which is having a life-partner.

In sum, as individuals, we can improve our lives by altering the manner in which we think about ourselves and the world. However, it needs to be kept in mind that many of these ideas and activities can have their downsides. Religiosity can lead to looking down on and denigrating people who do not share one's beliefs; while many religious faiths have this dark side, all have ideas that can promote happiness. Social groups with bonds within them can involve groups which exclude others as outsiders and seek to dominate them. Since these groups may well be an inescapable characteristic of societies, strengthening some groups by joining them can be a check on the power of other groups. Relationships with animals as pets can involve domination and status-related consumption, and nature activities can be destructive of nature. It is not the quantity of relationships— both in terms of the number of people (for instance, countless social media "friends") and time spent with them, but their quality and depth, that matters. Moreover, some "flow" activities, such as playing video games, can become addictive and result in unhappiness.

Solutions such as these may involve issues that are typically examined in different scholarly disciplines. For instance, volunteering to work on a political campaign might be thought of as a political act, thus subject to the domain of the political scientist, but at the same time is an act of community involvement, which concerns the sociologist and even the economist (though for some whom any volunteering would seem to involve both an immediate disutility as well as a collective action problem). Moreover, the solution to problems that arise from the economic and social sphere may well be found outside the normal boundaries of these social sciences, for example, through greater interest in spirituality, religion, or other causes greater than oneself that can help to reduce the importance given by people to status competition, which again underscores the importance of an interdisciplinary approach to the study of happiness.

Although it may be possible to take individual actions, these actions may be easier to engage in, and be more effective, when done with others and, in some cases, it may not be easy to sustain such action in an effective manner only at the individual level. One can develop suitable habits on one's own, meditate by oneself, and walk in nature alone. One can spend less money on things that do not provide gains that last by oneself, and work fewer hours unless money is required for necessities for one's family. In the economic sphere, for instance, one can try to work fewer hours and consume more carefully, but the social pressures to work more and engage in more status consumption may be too strong to overcome individually. Others, of course, must of necessity worker longer hours for purely financial reasons in more unsatisfying jobs than they might like, a point to which we return when considering other levels of analysis, suggesting as it does the need for collective solutions to problems such as low wages. In the political sphere, people may try to support particular policies, but whether these changes come to pass depends on what others do. Socially, one cannot join community organizations that do not exist, make friends when other people do not want to make friends, and spend more time with family members when others in the family have no time to do so.

The Group Level

Some of the problems that arise at the individual level can be overcome at the group level. Regarding the relationship between consumption and happiness, groups can overcome the problems faced by individuals in reducing and reorienting consumption in ways that can increase their happiness. For instance, people can form groups to help each other to overcome habits and addictions, an idea which is exploited by organizations such as Alcoholics Anonymous. Moreover, people can come together and agree (implicitly or explicitly) to not compete with each other through status consumption, creating consumption norms among themselves that reduce total consumption by them.

Regarding relationships between family members and friends, people can agree to spend more "quality" time together in ways that result in gains that last, implying higher levels of happiness. Latent groups can also, through the efforts of "entrepreneurial" individuals, come into being, transforming what might be solitary acts into communal ones—obvious examples include the idea of the book club or reading group, or, to borrow now the familiar metaphor from Putnam (2000), people can chose to form or join bowling leagues, rather than merely playing alone or with a single friend.

As we have discussed in prior chapters, and return to briefly below, labor unions are among the most important organizations in capitalist democracies. Much of the effect of unions is political, as reflected in the welfare state and other social democratic institutions that unions support, and which tend to improve quality of life for everyone (since, for instance, all workers become eligible for the minimum wage and unemployment insurance programs that unions tend to promote). That said, unions are potentially important in the lives of workers, providing as they do systems of emotional support and human connection—comradery—that is more likely to emerge in union shops. Unions also provide an immediate power resource for workers in the inevitable struggle between worker and employer, serving as a model example of how a group—a collection of working people banding together—can affect the world in ways that improve their well-being.

Although group level activities can overcome some of the problems associated with increasing happiness by individuals, it is, in many instances, difficult or even impossible for this to happen. Regarding consumption, it may be difficult for groups to change their consumption norms, which are at variance with norms that are followed by larger groups. It may be difficult to break addictions without government funding or interventions through taxes. Government policies which may increase average levels of happiness need to be adopted at state or even national levels; there is only so much that smaller groups of friends can do.

The National Level

Although some pro-happiness policies can be adopted through local government, many which aim to increase happiness or well-being may need to be undertaken at the national level (or, equivalently, at the provincial or state level in strong federalist systems).

Examples of such policies include those that impose limits on the length of the standard working day or over-time rules, work place safety regulations, pensions and benefits, and, above all, the decommodifying public policies that support a middle-class level of consumption, such as the minimum wage and income maintenance programs (that is, the welfare state). As was extensively documented in Chapter 3, it is the quality and universality of these programs that, perhaps more than anything else, determine quality of life across the world. As much as we wish to cling to the idea that happiness is mostly up to us as individuals, the reality is that, in large measure, the pursuit of happiness is a collective enterprise, in which the most vital task is building a society predicted on social solidarity.

There are, of course, potential problems with the institutions necessary to create such a society. It has been argued that these policies can create economic problems by, for instance, increasing government deficits to pay for them, and by raising wage costs that reduce profits for business. Thus, some argue, even if social democracy increases happiness now, it will cause economic problems in the long run by slowing down economic growth, by reducing profits, and by the state crowding out private investment. However, the policies in question can be financed through the taxation of high-income groups, and need not increase government debt. And even if the spending is financed by government borrowing, when unemployed resources exist in the economy, the expansion of aggregate demand due to these policies can increase profits, investment and growth. Similarly, an increase in wages at the lower end of income, by redistributing income from higher-income groups who save a higher fraction of their income to wage-earners who spend a higher proportion, aggregate demand is likely to increase. Higher wages can also lead to higher productivity growth, which can increase growth by increasing aggregate supply in economies where unemployment is at low levels.

All of these practices and policies, and many others besides, have historically depended upon organized labor. Labor unions appear to increase happiness both directly and indirectly via their impact on policy. To the extent that unions and the policies they favor do indeed promote happiness, innovations to make it easier for workers to organize may have a major long-term impact on quality of life. Indeed, the importance of organized labor is ever increasing, given that union membership is almost everywhere continuing decades of decline. As unions become weaker and weaker, and as fewer people benefit from their immediate protections or their indirect social benefits through public policy, quality of life will itself is likely to trend downward.

Tax policy is potentially equally important. Of particular interest is a proposal by Frank (1999) which replaces the U.S. income tax by a consumption tax. Frank's argument is that with a consumption tax people would be encouraged to save more and consume less than under the current income tax system, and there would also be a further negative effect on consumption to the extent that people consume more, for example for status reasons, when others consume more. Frank argues that such a tax could be made more progressive than the current income tax schedule to take into account the fact that people at lower levels of income have a higher propensity to consume than those at higher levels, and that the tax would not need the government to make arbitrary distinctions between necessities and luxuries and would tax only expenditures of the latter: people would themselves consume what they feel is more necessary. However, such a consumption tax may depress aggregate demand too much and cause unemployment unless people are willing to work fewer hours, and there is no guarantee that people will spend on the kinds of goods that satisfy more basic needs rather than those they want for ostentatious display. In fact, conspicuous consumption may be increased by making some goods more costly (with people having to pay higher consumption taxes).

It should also come as no surprise that people report increasing levels of subjective well-being with a cleaner environment, and well-being as measured by health indicators also improves with environmental improvements. Economists have for quite some time advocated economic solutions, such as effluent fees and environmental standards, to reduce environmental problems. Their approach has been to view environmental damage as a resulting form of externality in the sense that it affects others (more than the person causing the damage), and that economic actors do not take this negative externality into account in making their consumption and production decisions. Effluent taxes make polluters pay for the pollution they cause, and induce them to pollute less. Whether or not these efforts are effective, there is no doubt that big business and the military, and the adverse effects they have on the environment, require concerted state action.

These examples can be used to illustrate how solutions need to take into account issues examined by different disciplines. For instance, the consumption tax proposal takes into account the concerns of both economists (how taxes affect individual behavior and internalize consumption externalities because of which people do not take into account the effects of their consumption on the behavior of others, as in the pollution example) and sociologists (regarding status and social norms, for instance). Another example can be found by examining the effects of some tax and labor policies. A possible effect of the consumption tax is that it may reduce aggregate demand and increase unemployment, and it could reduce the willingness of people to work longer hours and thus increase their leisure time (although these two effects will work in opposite directions as far as the level of unemployment is concerned). The reduced incentive to work as well as direct policies to reduce the length of the working day can be expected to free up the time people have for other activities.

Such changes can create problems—obviously by raising the specter of unemployment—and also by increasing leisure time in which people have nothing enjoyable to do. The political support for government policies that maintain aggregate demand (which, of course, is a principal concern of organized labor, which has long pressed for full employment policies as well as more conventional strategies, such as generous unemployment compensation and more expansive job training, all of which maintain pressure on demand, and thus, employment) and that create conditions in which people can pursue enjoyable activities may well be necessary to overcome such problems.

The examples can also be used to illustrate that changes at different levels may be needed to solve some of the problems. For instance, it is possible that the consumption tax may make people—especially those with lower incomes—continue spending on status goods while reducing their expenditure on food and housing, thereby adversely affecting their health and security and, therefore, their well-being. They might do this because they may be overwhelmed by social pressures to consume, and because saving on food has adverse effects on health which may not be immediate. For this and other possible problems, solutions such as the consumption tax may not have their desirable effect, and could need to be supplemented by greater individual efforts to overcome the status motive. Moreover, economists may have been too quick to dismiss individual solutions to the problem of pollution by assuming that people only care about their private benefits and costs and not about how their activities affect others. By so doing, they unnecessarily limit their attention to taxes and standards, rather than supplementing such policies with efforts to inform people about the environmental consequences of their actions, which may well induce people to be more careful about damaging the environment.

These national changes cannot emerge in a vacuum. Powerful interests, including rich individuals and corporations, have often opposed policies that can result in increasing happiness for many (and perhaps all) because they believe they reduce their power and restrict their freedoms. Through their influence on the media and on education they can influence the views of others. To overcome such obstacles, individual and group actions are needed to become more informed about what can increase happiness for oneself and for others, be less concerned about themselves and losing their small advantages and more concerned about others, especially those who are less well-off than themselves, and to join social and political movements and to vote for these changes.

The Global Level

Some problems can be fully addressed only at the global level. An obvious example is the problem of global climate change, where efforts by one country to limit the damage it does to the environment may be nullified by the activities of people in other countries. The solution to such global problems, of which global warming is the most visible one, requires global agreements.

Another issue is that in a globalized world what happens in one country has effects far beyond its borders. For instance, efforts to reduce pollution through regulations in one country may simply induce production to shift to other countries in which environmental regulations are less stringent, often because these countries are less developed economically and do not have the resources or the capability to have appropriate regulations that are properly implemented. Moreover, increases in consumption norms in one country can, through what have been called international demonstration effects, affect consumption levels in other countries because of technological changes and the reduced costs of transport and communications.

In the political realm, global agreements may be needed to allow countries that choose to adopt policies that are designed to increase happiness and well-being to pursue their experiments without interference by rich countries that believe such policies are against their economic interests directly, or by influencing the policies of international organizations such as the World Bank, the International Monetary Fund and the World Trade Organization (WTO).

These institutions take us to a final concern: economic globalization itself. We have already reviewed in this volume the role of the welfare state and similar political interventions in the market for the benefit of workers, which appear to support higher levels of well-being. Globalization generally, and often via the auspices of the Bretton Woods institutions specifically, makes the maintenance of such programs ever more difficult. The same international competition for low-cost labor places similar downward pressure on the ability of workers to organize. To be sure, globalization is a complicated phenomenon, likely to produce different sets of winners and losers, improving some conditions in some places, but having the opposite effects in others. It may well be that future generations may see the process as positively transformative, the costs of which, like those that accompanied the end of feudalism, having proved necessary for a better future. That said, however, it seems likely that globalization will, at least for the foreseeable future, decrease the overall level of well-being of many people in the world by weakening the two central institutions (the welfare state and the labor union) that insulate citizens against the insecurity created by market fluctuations. This may be doubly so, when we take into consideration that the increase in consumption that globalization is argued to provide may well not result in more happiness, for reasons now familiar. Thus, even if the advocates of globalization prove to be correct in their judgment (itself passionately disputed by opponents) that the process will eventually result in a more equitable and even richer world in terms of material goods, well-being and happiness may still decline.

If so, citizens of the world need to confront not only the direct negative effects of globalization, such as environmental destruction, but to face more directly the human costs of the process of globalization itself, insofar as globalization threatens to destroy those <u>decommodifying institutions</u> that protect individuals against market forces that are, by their very nature, indifferent to the fate of human beings and of life on earth itself.

Further Reading

Alvarez-Diaz, Á.; Gonzalez, L.; Radcliff, B. (2010). *The Politics of Happiness: On the Political Determinants of Quality of Life in the American States*. The Journal of Politics 72 (3): 894-905.

Aristotle (350 BCE). Nicomachean Ethics. Translated by Ross, W.D. McKeon, R. (Ed.) *In The Basic Works of Aristotle*. Random House: New York (1941).

Ben-Shahar, T. (2007). *Happier*. McGraw-Hill: New York.

Bourdieu, P. (1986). The Forms of Capital. Richardson, J. (Ed.) *Handbook of Theory and Research in the Sociology of Education*. Greenwood: New York.

Brown, S.; Taylor, K.; Price, S. W. (Eds.) (2005). *Debt and distress: Evaluating the psychological cost of credit*. Journal of Economic Psychology, 26: 642-61.

David, S.; Boniwell I.; Ayers, A. C. (Eds.) (2013). *Oxford Handbook of Happiness*. Oxford University Press: Oxford.

Demir, M.; Weitekamp, L. A. (2007). *I am So Happy 'Cause Today I Found My Friend: Friendship and Personality as Predictors of Happiness*. Journal of Happiness Studies 8 (2): 181-211.

Dutt, A. K. (2009). *Happiness and the Relative Consumption Hypothesis.* Dutt, A. K.; Radcliff, B. (Eds.) *Happiness, Economics and Politics. Towards a multidisciplinary approach.* Edward Elgar: Cheltenham.

Dutt, A. K.; Radcliff, B. (2009). *What is to be Done.* Dutt, A. K.; Radcliff, B (Eds.) *Happiness, Economics and Politics.* Edward Elgar: Cheltenham.

Easterlin, R. (1973). *Does Economic Growth Improve the Human Lot? Some Empirical Evidence.* David, P.; Reder, M. (Eds.) *Nations and Households in Economic Growth.* Stanford University Press: Palo Alto.

Easterlin, R. (2001). *Income and Happiness: Towards a Unified Theory.* Economic Journal, 111: 465-84.

Easwaran, E. (1987). *The Upanishads.* Nilgiri Press: Berkeley.

Ferrer-i-Carbonell, A.; Gowdy, J. M. (2007). *Environmental degradation and happiness.* Ecological economics, 60 (3): 509-516.

Flavin, P.; Pacek, A.; Radcliff, B. (2010). *Labor Unions and Life Satisfaction: Evidence from New Data.* Social Indicators Research 98 (2): 435-499.

Frank, R. (1999). *Luxury Fever. Why Money Fails to Satisfy in an Era of Excess.* The Free Press: New York.

Frey, B. S.; Stutzer, A. (2002). *Happiness and Economics*. Princeton University Press: Princeton.

Galbraith, J. K. (1958). *The Affluent Society*. Hamilton: London.

Haybron, D. M. (2008). *The Pursuit of Unhappiness. The elusive psychology of well-being*. Oxford University Press: Oxford and New York.

Hidaka, B. H. (2012). *Depression as a disease of modernity: explanations for increasing prevalence*. Current Neurology and Neuroscience Reports, U.S. National Library of Medicine.

Hirsch, F. (1976). *Social Limits Growth*. Harvard University Press: Cambridge.

Kahneman, D. (1999). *Objective Happiness*. Kahneman, D.; Diener, E.; Schwarz, N. (Eds.) *Well-Being: The Foundations of Hedonic Psychology*. Russell Sage Foundation: New York.

Kahneman, D.; Deaton, A. (2010). *High income improves evaluation of life but not emotional well-being*. Proceedings of the National Academy of Sciences 107 (38): 16489-16493.

Kasser, T. (2002). *The High Price of Materialism*. MIT Press: Cambridge.

Lambin, E. (2012). *An Ecology of Happiness.* University of Chicago Press: Chicago.

Layard, R. (2005). Happiness. *Lessons from a New Science.* Penguin Press: London.

Lyubomirsky, S. (2007). *The How of Happiness: A New Approach to Getting the Life you Want.* Penguin Random House: New York.

Maslow, A. H. (1943). *A Theory of Human Motivation.* Psychological Review: 37-96.

Matsubayashi T; Ueda M. (2012). *Government Partisanship and Human Well-Being.* Social Indicators Research 107 (1): 127-148.

McMahon, D. M. (2006). *Happiness. A History.* Atlantic Monthly Press: New York.

Mill, J. S. (1873). *Autobiography.* Longman, Green, Reader and Dyer: London.

Nettle, D. (2005). *Happiness. The Science Behind Your Smile.* Oxford University Press: Oxford.

O'Connor, K. (2017). *Happiness and Welfare State Policy Around the World.* Review of Behavioral Economics 4 (4): 397-420.

Okulicz-Kozaryn, A.; Holmes O.; Avery, D. (2014). *The Subjective Well-Being Political Paradox: Happy Welfare States and Unhappy Liberals.* Journal of Applied Psychology, 99 (6): 1300-1308.

Pacek, A.; Radcliff, B. (2008). *Assessing the Welfare State.* Perspectives on Politics 6 (2): 267-277.

Polanyi, K. (1944). *The great transformation.* Beacon Press: Boston.

Putnam, R. (2000). *Bowling Alone. The Collapse and Revival of American Community.* Touchstone Books: New York.

Radcliff, B.; Radcliff, A. (1993). *Understanding Zen.* Charles Tuttle: Boston.

Radcliff, B. (2013). *Political Economy of Human Happiness.* Cambridge University Press: Cambridge and New York.

Rehdanz, K.; Maddison, D. (2005). *Climate and Happiness.* Ecological Economics, 52 (1): 111-125.

Schor, J. (1998). *The Overspent American. Upscaling, Downshifting and the New Consumer.* Basic Books: New York.

Scitovsky, T. (1976). *The Joyless Economy. An Inquiry into Human Satisfaction and Consumer Dissatisfaction.* Oxford University Press: Oxford.

Scruggs, L.; Detlef, J.; Kuitto, K. (2017). *Comparative Welfare Entitlements Dataset 2. Version 2017-09.* University of Connecticut and University of Greifswald.

Sen, A. K. (1999). *Development as Freedom.* Anchor Books: New York.

Senik, C. (2005). *Income distribution and well-being: what can we learn from subjective data?* Journal of Economic Surveys, 19 (1): 43-63.

Smith, A. (1776). *An Inquiry into the Nature and Causes of the Wealth of Nations.* W. Strahan and T. Cadell: London.

Stevenson, B.; Wolfers, J. (2008). *Economic Growth and Subjective Well-Being: Reassessing the Easterlin Paradox.* Brookings Papers on Economic Activity, Spring: 1-87.

Stiglitz, J. (1994). *Whither Socialism?* MIT Press: Boston.

Stiglitz, J. (2015). *The Welfare State in the Twenty First Century*. Paper presented at Columbia University conference on *The Welfare State and the Fight Against Inequality*. November 8-9, 2015.

Tuttle, C. (2001). *Child Labor during the British Industrial Revolution*. Whaples, R. (Ed.) EH. Net Encyclopedia: August 14.

Ulrich, R. S. (1984). *View through a window may influence recovery from surgery*. Science 224 (4647): 420-421.

Veblen, T. (1899). *The Theory of the Leisure Class. An Economic Study of Institutions*. Macmillan: London and New York.

Veenhoven, R. (1996). *Developments in Satisfaction Research*. Social Indicators Research 37 (1): 1-46.

Veenhoven, R. (2009). *How do we assess how happy we are?* Dutt, A. K.; Radcliff, B. (Eds.) *Happiness, Economics, Politics*. Edward Elgar: Celthenham.

Warr, P. (1999). *Well-being and the Workplace*. Kahneman, D.; Diener, E.; Schwarz, N. (Eds.) *Well-Being: The Foundations of Hedonic Psychology*. Russell Sage Foundation: New York.

Welsch, H. (2006). *Environment and happiness: Valuation of air pollution using life satisfaction data.* Ecological economics, 58 (4): 801-813.

Wilson, E. O. (1984). *Biophilia.* Harvard University Press: Cambridge.

Wilson, E. G. (2008). *Against Happiness: In Praise of Melancholy.* Farrar, Straus and Giroux: New York.

CPSIA information can be obtained
at www.ICGtesting.com
Printed in the USA
LVHW082236260220
648357LV00018B/829